SCHOOLS FOR THE SIXTIES

A Report of the Project on Instruction
NATIONAL EDUCATION ASSOCIATION

McGRAW-HILL BOOK COMPANY
New York   London   Toronto

This symbol of the Project on Instruction combines a legacy of the past (π for $\pi\alpha\iota\delta\epsilon\acute{\iota}\alpha$, the ancient Greek word for education) with direction for the future (), which the Project seeks to identify.

II

Schools for the Sixties

Library of Congress Catalog Card Number: 63-21503

Beginning with the gathering of 43 educators in Philadelphia in August 1857, the organized profession has given high priority to curriculum and instruction. The Project on Instruction is one of several major efforts sponsored by the National Education Association in this century to upgrade the quality of American education and to give it direction. These have included the 1918 statement of the "Seven Cardinal Principles" of education by the NEA's Commission on the Reorganization of Secondary Education, and the 1938 and 1961 Educational Policies Commission statements on *The Purposes of Education in American Democracy* and *The Central Purpose of American Education.*

The publication of this volume continues the Association's commitment in this area. The Project on Instruction has been supported from its beginning by the funds of the National Education Association. It has profited from endeavor among NEA departments and units. The departments and units are exploring further ways of using findings of the Project and ways of moving forward to other cooperative enterprises.

Many people have joined with the NEA in this effort: elementary and secondary school teachers, school administrators, scholars in the academic disciplines, university professors of education, and distinguished laymen. Their interest and willing cooperation have been impressive testimony to a shared concern for improvements in learning. The NEA is grateful for this valuable contribution to the Project on Instruction. Appendix C of this volume names many more of the people who have assisted than can be listed here.

The wise guidance given to the Project by the National Committee and its Director and staff calls for special recognition.

WILLIAM G. CARR
Executive Secretary, NEA

MELVIN W. BARNES, *Chairman*
National Committee
Project on Instruction

FROM MANY
VOICES

Education in the United States can be as good as the citizens of this country want it to be—and no better. The basic commitment to good education must come from the people. Granted such a commitment, there is a fundamental question that must be raised and answered—and raised again: What is good education?

Sound decisions about the kind of education that is good for a given people at a given time in history rest upon information that is pertinent and accurate, upon thinking that is rational and objective, and upon values that are clear and compelling. Today a special urgency dictates educational reappraisal and anticipates educational change. This urgency stems from three basic but complex sets of facts:

1. Contemporary society is changing fundamentally and rapidly. It is changing so fundamentally and so rapidly that we have difficulty fitting ourselves into the present and projecting ourselves into the future. We, and the oncoming generations, must look to the schools for help in understanding, living with, and directing social change. "We cannot, any more than could past generations, see the face of the future," says Ralph McGill. "But we know that written across it is the word education."[1]

2. The almost incredible explosion of knowledge threatens to overwhelm us unless we can find, and quickly, some intel-

ligent solutions to problems created by the new and growing wealth of information. What knowledge to select and how to organize it for learning—these are two of the problems that require continuing attention.

3. Significant discoveries are being made about people and learning—discoveries that emphasize the vast range of differences among and within individuals and point to the great variety of ways in which people can learn. At a time when there is so much to be learned, and so urgent a need to learn it, we must create new teaching methods and adapt old ones to accelerate and enrich the teaching-learning process.

These facts of our twentieth-century life—a rapidly changing society, a mounting store of knowledge, and new understandings about people and about learning—create some basic problems relating to the instructional program of the schools. There is no shortage of ideas about what these problems are and how they should be solved. There is, in fact, a constant babble of voices as millions of people with many and often conflicting ideas speak out about education.

Many of the voices call for a return to the "solid subjects." Some would prescribe the same program for all pupils, regardless of individual differences. Some would ignore what is known about the ways children learn. And some would express concern only for more and more attention to their particular subject.

Some of the voices come from outside the profession. Some come from within the profession at the university level of academic and professional scholarship. And many come from leaders in elementary and secondary education.

All of these voices have a right to be heard. One voice that should speak out clearly indeed is the voice of the teaching profession itself. With this firm belief, the National Education Association established in 1959 the Project on the Instructional Program of the Public Schools (Project on Instruction). To this Project it gave a major task: make thoughtful and creative recommendations to serve as a guide to the profession and the public in their combined efforts to study and improve the quality of the instructional program in the schools.

A fourteen-member National Committee and a headquarters staff were appointed to carry on the work of the Project. The National Committee was composed of classroom teachers, public school administrators, and university professors. From time to time, distinguished citizens and scholars in the academic disciplines served in special advisory capacities.

Early in its deliberations, the Committee examined its role as a spokesman for the organized teaching profession. The members agreed unanimously that the Committee's function was not to respond to the "critics," nor to enunciate a "national curriculum," nor to recommend specific content. Rather, the Committee decided it could make the most significant contribution by identifying critical concerns in American education and formulating recommendations about them.

Inevitably, limits had to be set for the scope of the Project. These limits were set in terms of the timeliness of the issues, the feasibility of their resolution, and the desire not to duplicate significant work already completed or now in progress by other groups. In addition, it was determined that an analysis of a few crucial decision areas was more in keeping with the Project's goals than a generalized approach would be. Thus, issues related to pupil or staff evaluation, teacher education, and matters dealing directly with the teaching act were not given major attention.

Three major tasks, then, gave structure to the Project: identification and clarification of instructional issues or questions, development of recommendations about the issues, and explanation of the reasoning used to arrive at the recommendations. In the identification process, two categories—"Deciding What To Teach" and "Planning and Organizing for Teaching"—emerged to become the focus of intensive study. For analysis of these issues, Project participants used three sources of data: the academic disciplines; social forces and trends, including the status of present instructional practices in the schools; and the research in human growth and development and the psychology of learning. Twelve specific decision areas were identified; twelve questions were asked about the instructional program. The Committee is on record that, within the limits set by the Project, these are the important questions about which decisions should be made.

These twelve questions and thirty-three recommendations related to them are discussed in *Schools for the Sixties*, which is the official report of the National Committee of the NEA Project on Instruction. This report is directed to school-board members, to other interested citizens who influence decisions about education, and to our colleagues in the teaching profession. Careful reading of the Committee's recommendations is urged, but the reader is cautioned to read more than just the recommendations. In most cases the questions raised and the supporting material are critical to clear and complete understanding.

Schools for the Sixties is one of a series of four reports published by the Project. It summarizes what is included in greater depth in three supporting volumes—*Deciding What To Teach, Planning and Organizing for Teaching,* and *Education in a Changing Society.*[2] Those persons interested in the fullest understanding of the Project's work are encouraged to delve into these three supporting volumes in which close attention is given to the critical questions that are summarized in this publication. *Schools for the Sixties* borrows heavily from its original sources, and the authors have been paraphrased or quoted exactly whenever possible. This material is not footnoted in the usual manner because of the close interrelationship among all the volumes.

Schools for the Sixties has a preface and four chapters. "From Many Voices" describes the Project and its purposes. Chapter 1 discusses data for decisions and then focuses on the question, "Who should make what decisions about education?" It also makes recommendations about research, experimentation, and innovation. Chapter 2 discusses the issues and recommendations related to "Deciding What To Teach." Chapter 3 reports the issues and recommendations related to "Planning and Organizing for Teaching." Chapter 4 previews the future—suggests directions for American education and some actions that can be taken by school boards, other interested citizens, and the teaching profession. Some duplication exists among the chapters. The duplication is deliberate; it is essential for clear exploration of important ideas common to several issues.

No one on the National Committee anticipates or particularly desires complete agreement with all of the recommendations. Had such agreement been the goal, the result would have been a bland document filled with innocuous platitudes that might evoke mild "amens" but would be unlikely to move anyone to action—even at the armchair level of verbal support or disagreement.

If some recommendations are at odds with beliefs firmly held by other equally conscientious educators, what must be resolved is not the integrity of the individuals who agree or disagree, but the validity of the beliefs themselves. An objective search for reliable answers to basic questions in education is a continuing need. Such a search should be conducted with the certain but not discouraging knowledge that some of the answers will be validated, some will be disproved, and some will be supplanted by others.

It is obvious that there are no easy, final answers to important problems of curriculum and instruction. There are no quick, black-and-white solutions for them. Let us be clear that our recommendations will make a difference in the decision-making of America's schools only if they are used as a guide for self-study, not if they are adopted without careful thought.

Not long ago, a well-known writer on education compared committee reports to the chorus in a Greek drama: too many of them give warning of vague trials ahead without interfering with the business of the actors or killing the suspense of the audience. Choruses and committees may be vocal without being particularly helpful to theater-goers and report-readers. It is well, however, to keep in mind that a committee report is not an aesthetic substitute for action, but, hopefully, a stimulus to it. The National Committee will be happy to excuse itself from the Greek chorus if its report stimulates intelligent and spirited conversation about significant questions in education and if that conversation leads on to action that makes a difference in the schools of America.

Ole Sand, *Director*
Richard I. Miller, *Associate Director*   ix

The principal writers of this volume were: Robert J. Havighurst, Professor of Education, University of Chicago; Dorothy Neubauer, Associate Executive Secretary, Department of Elementary School Principals, NEA; and Margery Thompson, Program Specialist, Project on Instruction, NEA. Ole Sand and Richard I. Miller contributed staff guidance and wrote portions of the manuscript.

TABLE OF CONTENTS

xi

Chapter 1

THE RIGHT
QUESTIONS

Americans are often characterized—sometimes accusingly—as a restless people, on the move, who put great emphasis on the new and different, who welcome change. In many ways this is true. We do move around—across the country and up the ladder—and our history is threaded with examples of new challenges met in a "can do" spirit with a zest for the unknown. We have found this rewarding spiritually and materially and we tend, therefore, to equate change with change for the better—often the sooner the better. We question it sometimes but like to think we are adaptable, particularly when the chips are down.

This dynamic image is often in ironic contrast to other facts of life in America. One is that a democracy is not the most efficient form of government for instituting or implementing rapid change. No one person makes the decisions; millions do. The same is true of the large complex organizations which are more and more dominant in our society. Few executives, no matter how strong, can direct corporations or industries single-handed; too many people are involved in too many ways. The challenges today are great, many of them are ill-defined, most of them defy quick solution. People, even countries, acknowledge the need for sustained group effort. We no longer quickly mobilize for a war, win it, and go home; we work at agreements and cooperative action with other countries to keep the peace over a long pull.

In an enterprise as vast as our educational system, the decisions made and the changes supported reflect our inclination to get on with the job, and our impatience for quick results. But what "results" do we want? What do we expect from education? Goodlad has said:[3]

> The tasks of education are profoundly complex. Man has rocketed his kind into space. He has brought back into pulsating life a human being already pronounced dead. He has fashioned in his own likeness robots that remember, file, sort, and then answer in moments problems that would tax a hundred men for a thousand days. But men still cheat and steal and kill as they did a thousand years ago and thousands of years before that.
>
> These are not always trapped men or hungry men or threatened men who cheat and steal and kill. Some men pronounced learned cheat because they are vain. Some men pronounced holy steal because they are greedy. Some men pronounced wise kill because they have established no identity with their fellow men. The people who soon may bring down upon themselves a holocaust are—or will have been—the most educated of all time.

No man is just *educated;* he is educated for something, for some purpose, for many purposes. Decisions about the purposes of education and about ways to achieve these purposes are made by many people—and should be. But before good decisions can be made, the right questions must be asked. And before the right questions can be asked, the areas of concern must be identified. A major task of the NEA Project on Instruction was to identify significant areas of concern, select from these areas the ones on which the Project would concentrate, and then raise the right questions about them. Realistically, the framework of the Project did not lend itself to thorough treatment of all of the significant areas in education. Limits had to be set, with the result that certain significant concerns—pupil and teacher evaluation, teacher education, and the teaching act itself, for example—are not treated in any detail.

Twelve areas of educational concern were identified—matters about which decisions need to be made—and a cluster of questions about them were formulated. The decision areas and the questions are these:

DECISION AREA I   Decision-Making

Who should make what decisions about education?

DECISION AREA II   Research, Experimentation, and Innovation

How can an extensive program of educational research, experimentation, and innovation be developed?

DECISION AREA III   Educating All Children and Youth

How can the instructional program of the school be designed to develop the individual potentialities of all members of the school population within the framework of a society that values both unity and diversity?

DECISION AREA IV   Establishing Priorities for the School

What are the distinctive responsibilities of the school in contrast to those that are distinctive to the family, the church, industry, and various youth-serving agencies?

What responsibilities should the school share with other institutions and with other youth-serving agencies?

What, then, should be included in the school program?

What should be excluded from it?

3

DECISION AREA V — The School's Role in Dealing with National Problems Related to Youth

What is the school's role in dealing with serious national problems such as youth unemployment and juvenile delinquency?

DECISION AREA VI — Teaching About Controversial Issues and About Communism

What is the school's role in teaching about controversial issues and about communism and other ideologies?

DECISION AREA VII — A Balanced Program

How can the school provide a balanced program for the individual and maintain it amidst various pressures for specialization?

DECISION AREA VIII — Selecting Content

How can schools make wise selections of content from the ever-growing body of available knowledge?

DECISION AREA IX — Organizing Content

How should the content of the curriculum be organized?

DECISION AREA X   Organizing the Curriculum

How should the curriculum of the school be organized to give appropriate direction to the instructional process?

DECISION AREA XI   Organizing the School and the Classroom

How should the school and the classroom be organized to make the most effective use of the time and talents of students and teachers?

DECISION AREA XII   Instructional Materials, Technology, Space

How can the quality of instructional materials be improved? How can the products of modern technology be used effectively? How can space be designed and used to support the instructional program?

5

The terms "issues," "questions," and "decision areas" are used interchangeably throughout this report, although their definitions are not precisely the same. In a general sense, they refer to the preceding list which formed the core of the Committee's concerns.

DATA FOR DECISIONS

Decisions cannot be made in a vacuum. The questions posed in this report can be resolved only on the basis of a deliberate analysis of the forces which shape education.

In formulating its recommendations, the Committee has sought direction from three major sources: social trends and forces, knowledge of the human being as a learner, and the accumulated body of organized knowledge about the world and man. In these areas are the forces which determine the setting and the possible method and substance of education. These forces must then be screened against the values and objectives which society sets for education, the guides which influence the translation of what could be into what shall be.

These bases for decision—values, objectives, the society, the learner, and organized knowledge—are constant in the sense that each must be considered whenever and wherever fundamental educational decisions are made. But they are also changeable, for times and people change, evolving different data for educational decision making.

The following sections—"A Statement of Values," "Essential Objectives of Education," "Society as a Base," "The Learner as a Base," "Organized Knowledge as a Base"[4]—summarize the Committee's appraisal of these major considerations and briefly review the reasoning underlying its recommendations.

A Statement of Values

Every society is directed and sustained by a core of values which represents its ideals, its standards, and its norms of what is desirable. There are also, in every society, values which are a reflection of human preferences, of what people actually want and seek to obtain. These operational values develop from personal needs and sometimes conflict with the society's normative values; what people *do* want is not always consistent with what they believe they *ought* to want.

Today, the racial situation in our country points up such an inconsistency. Freedom, justice, equality have always been ideals of America; as citizens, we pledge allegiance in the words "with liberty and justice for all." Yet, lack of freedom, injustice, and great inequalities exist in this country because personal values about race and religion, bolstered by custom and habit, override the patriotic ideals of many of our people.

Actual wants are modified by changes in society and culture. Today people value many things which earlier generations did not, simply because these objects of desire did not exist as genuine possibilities. Values in terms of material comforts are quite different than they were before the fruits of mass production and technology were available. Values in terms of attitudes and behavior will change as more and more people, Negro and white, recognize that traditional roles cannot forever be maintained comfortably.

Educational values should, and do, reflect the generally accepted ideals of society. Our standards of what ought to be should be a guide to both teaching and learning. Equally necessary, educational values should reflect the needs and interests of the learner. Education must comprehend what *is* before it can broaden and relate the immediate to the ideal. The educator's task is to build continuity between the interests of the learner and the standards of excellence which transcend the immediate desires of the immature.

The values against which the multiple possibilities for educational practice are screened must be made explicit. To do otherwise would be to make decisions without reference to what we seek to obtain and without sufficient heed to the actual needs of those for whom we seek to obtain it. The National Committee believes that the following values are vital as criteria for assessing present practices and as guides to future improvement of our common schools:

- respect for the worth and dignity of every individual
- equality of opportunity for all children

- encouragement of variability
- faith in man's ability to make rational decisions
- shared responsibility for the common good
- respect for moral and spiritual values and ethical standards of conduct

Essential Objectives of Education

The schools should not, and cannot, provide all of the learning opportunities that students need in order to live fully and effectively. Other agencies have particular responsibilities in the education of youth and learning also takes place outside of the school—and continuously throughout life. Furthermore, school time and facilities are finite, making it impossible, as well as undesirable, that the schools be the source for all necessary learning.

Education is a process of changing behavior—behavior in the broad sense of thinking, feeling, and acting. As a result of education, students should acquire ideas they did not have, skills they did not possess, interests broader and more mature than they had known, ways of thinking more effective than they had employed. From this viewpoint, educational objectives may be stated in terms of behavioral change, and the responsibilities of the schools may be differentiated from those of other educative agencies.

It is necessary for the schools to choose relatively few important objectives, to work toward them consistently, and to review them periodically in the light of changing times. The additive approach—putting more subject-matter areas into the curriculum and adopting a multitude of educational goals—is ineffective.

The basic criterion in establishing priorities should be an assessment of the contributions which education can make to the individual, to our society, and to the improvement of mankind. In this swift-moving world, such choices are not easy. What knowledge will today's ten-year-old need three decades hence? What skills will he require to live successfully? What problems will he have to solve? In what social context will he need to reinterpret basic human values? Education must help the individual to identify and maintain values that are relatively constant. It also must equip him to cope with change.

The essential objectives of education, therefore, must be premised on a recognition that education is a process of changing behavior and that a changing society requires the capacity for self-teaching and self-adaptation. Priorities in educational objectives should be placed upon such ends as:

- learning how to learn, how to attack new problems, how to acquire new knowledge
- using rational processes
- building competence in basic skills
- developing intellectual and vocational competence
- exploring values in new experience
- understanding concepts and generalizations

Above all, the school must develop in the pupil the ability to learn under his own initiative and an abiding interest in doing so.

Society as a Base

The Committee reviewed dominant forces in contemporary society in an effort to anticipate some of the social changes which will create a new setting for education—changes which need to be comprehended in making educational decisions. The forces are: science and technology, economic growth, large bureaucratic organizations, leisure time, television and other mass media, urbanization, population growth, and international interdependence and conflict. Discussion of these forces is interwoven throughout this report in the brief analyses of the Committee's recommendations. They are also dealt with in the Project's three supporting volumes; specific attention is paid to each force in one of the volumes, *Education in a Changing Society.*[5]

The forces mentioned above are apparent not only in our own country but throughout the world, particularly those concerning economic growth, population growth, and the cold war. One of the most fundamental changes that is occurring in the world— the effort of the colored races to throw off the dominance of the white race—is accelerated by and transcends many of the forces listed. This change is manifested in Africa and Asia by the number of new nations rapidly carved from former colonies and by their rejection of white leadership; here, at home, it is apparent in the increasing vigor of the Negroes' struggle for equal civil rights and in their impatience with gradualism.

These changes affect the lives of students profoundly; an intelligent awareness of them is only the beginning toward shaping them to positive rather than negative effects. The schools cannot correct housing patterns, employment practices, voting registration laws any more than they can alter the bitter residue of a "white-man's-burden" colonial policy or call back the scientific discoveries that presage man's control—or destruction—of nature. But the schools can help students to gain a knowledge of the world in which they find themselves, with a more complete history of all its cultures and as many possible solutions to its problems as mortal men can now foresee. This much, *at the very least,* the schools can and should do.

The Learner as a Base

An important fact, which is not always easily recognized by educators, is that every child has an inner push to become a more complete self, to learn what can become meaningful to him. The art of teaching lies in stimulating this force and in keeping it alive, free, and developing. To do so, it is essential to understand the learner, to know what he is working on, what he is up against, what his basic assets are.

Investigations by psychologists during the last fifteen years have provided much significant information about thinking, learning, and personality. Their findings are helping to lay a better foundation for changes in curriculum and methods of teaching. Today there is a closer connection between psychology and the practice of education than there has been for many years, and more academicians are becoming interested in ways children learn.

It seems clear now that development is achieved through learning, probably constrained by biochemical processes that probably in some sense are genetically regulated. The idea of development as emergence according to a precise timetable is withering on the vine. Most forward-looking psychologists now see the child not as the innocent victim of society but as the creative product of society. It is appropriate in our society to consider education as a demand upon the individual rather than as a privilege or as therapy. Progress and happiness can both be served, it is conceded, when adults get behind the child and push. There can be both excellence and mental health provided we do not go overboard, letting the push become abuse, and believing that mind is everything.[6]

Some of the concerns that seem most significant in educational planning and practice, in terms of the learner, are:

- recognizing and nurturing creativity
- promoting the development of responsibility
- promoting the development of positive self-attitudes
- relating learning to development in children
- evaluating the learner's motivations
- acknowledging inter-individual differences
- acknowledging intra-individual differences
- acknowledging social-group differences

Organized Knowledge as a Base

Probably the most important single factor forcing change upon education is the explosion of knowledge—the "information revolution." Furthermore, because scientific and scholarly work is now quite extensive and many people are engaged in it, the rate of revision is swift. Teaching the disciplines in this situation clearly requires teaching something more permanent and more pervasive than a catalogue of factual knowledge, although some facts are essential, and it is clear that there is a continuing need for drill and repetition for learning of basic information.

Educators are not only concerned with the *amount of knowledge* students possess but also with students' *lack of understanding* about what they presumably know. Since about 1955, a vivid awareness of this latter problem has led some scholars and re- 11 searchers to explore ways of selecting, organizing, and teaching available information to make it more intelligible and more usable. In general, the recent studies shift the balance in learning from *inventory* to *transaction*. The structure of a discipline, its methods of inquiry, and the styles of thinking of its scholars and specialists offer important keys to this educational task.

Developing structure in generalizations, rules, and styles of thought in the elementary and secondary school curriculum requires the talents of the teacher or curriculum worker as much as those of specialists in the academic disciplines. It imposes a great responsibility on the teacher to keep current with the frontiers of knowledge, even though the general principles best learned by pupils may be broader and simpler than those of specialists.

These approaches to organized knowledge are analyzed in detail in Chapter 2 in the discussion of content selection and content organization.

The first two decision areas of the dozen listed as central concerns of the Project on Instruction are related, as are the data for decisions, to each of the other areas. Whatever question is to be resolved, roles and responsibilities must be clear: "Who makes what decisions about education?" Wherever educational improvements are anticipated, research, experimentation, and innovation are essential. "How can an extensive program of educational research, experimentation, and innovation be developed?" The discussion of these two questions is, therefore, presented in this chapter, preceding consideration of the other ten decision areas.

DECISION AREA I   Decision-Making

Who should make what decisions about education?

Decisions about what to teach, how to teach, and how to organize for teaching are made daily. Many people are involved in the process. All are entitled, by virtue of their citizenship in a democracy, to make certain kinds of decisions; some are authorized by law to make other kinds. Some are qualified by education, experience, and position to make still other decisions. The quality and validity of the judgments that are made depend, in part, upon clarification and observance of the differing roles of the various people involved.

Decisions that affect the instructional program are made at three levels of remoteness from the student. Close to the students, teachers make daily *instructional* decisions. At a more remote level, teachers and administrators make *institutional* decisions. At a still more remote level, school-board members, state legislators, and federal officials make *societal* educational decisions.

At the instructional level, teachers plan units of work, select materials, set up learning situations. At the institutional level, teachers and administrators determine specific curricular sequences, ways of relating the various subject-fields, and systems of moving students upward through the school. At the societal level, school boards determine, for example, whether or not to have special programs for the partially deaf and whether or not to provide funds for closed-circuit television. At a still more remote level, legislators and state school-board members ponder problems of organizing and financing elementary, secondary, and higher education, and of technical, sectarian, and correspondence schools. The decisions of federal and state governments about such matters as providing school lands, defending the rights of minority groups, and specifying minimum requirements support some educational activities and restrict others.

Educational decisions at each level are influenced by available knowledge and by the values used in its selection. Continuous improvement of the instructional program demands that the most relevant knowledge be brought to bear as precisely as possible at each decision-making point.

Educational decisions are influenced also by formal and informal political structure. Federal and state governments enact legislation and vote funds for educational purposes; powerful vested-interest groups lobby to block or expedite legislative action; some individuals and some groups influence school practice in various ways. School boards deliberate over the suggestions and criticisms of groups and individuals attending their meetings, but members may be even more responsive to the influence of between-meeting associations.

Many citizens, teachers included, sometimes lack awareness and understanding of the powerful informal determinants of educational policy and practice. Authority to make instructional decisions is in the hands of state and local educational officials, but many powerful external forces influence the decisions. As vested-interest groups grow larger and more powerful, the comparative weakness of local authorities in giving direction to education becomes more apparent. The state governments in which the legal responsibility for education is vested in our system do not always assume strong leadership. There is a compensating tendency for federal participation and authority to increase, especially when state responsibility is not assumed vigorously. Today this tendency toward centralization is accelerated by the recognized significance of education in ultimate survival.

Does this mean that the tradition of local-state control of the school curriculum has outlived its usefulness in today's national community? Is local control in reality a myth, destroyed in substance though not in form by influences that are nationwide in their operation? Should the reality be acknowledged and dealt with by vesting legal authority for instructional decisions in a national agency, either governmental or professional?

These questions, which are discussed in the Project volume *Deciding What To Teach*, lead directly to the basic issue: *Who should make instructional decisions for the public schools today?* They point up the need to reduce the discrepancies between what *has been* the traditional picture, what *is* the actual practice in making educational decisions, and what *should be* the practice in the 1960s and the 1970s.

The question then becomes: *Who* should make *what* decisions about education? The answer, in each case, depends on the nature of the decision to be made and the kinds of information required to make it intelligently. The National Committee for the Project on Instruction makes five recommendations in the area of decision making.

14

RECOMMENDATION 1 *Local school boards are the legal instruments through which the state fulfills its responsibility for education. The distinction between lay control of school policies determined by the board of education and implementation of these policies by the professional staff, with the leadership of the local superintendent, should be delineated, understood, and respected.*

Local school boards

The tradition of local responsibility for education is deeply rooted in American traditions. As early as 1642 and 1647, the Massachusetts Bay Colony passed laws requiring each town to provide schools to teach children writing and religion, and to pay for these schools out of town funds. These early laws established two precedents that have remained with American education: the right of the state to require local communities to provide for publicly supported education, and the right of the local community to determine its own educational framework within the context of state and national laws.

Extensive powers to operate the schools, within the framework of state education laws, are vested in the local boards of education. These laws vary from state to state. In some cases, decisions are left almost entirely to the local school system; in others, the state prescribes many parts of the program. Although there are exceptions in some statutory curriculum prescriptions, the requirements tend to be so general that major responsibility for specific curriculum developments rests with the local school system.

The complementary but distinct roles of the lay board of education and the professional staff of the school should be delineated, understood, and respected. The board of education should make decisions about policies. The implementation of those policies is the responsibility of the professional staff with the leadership of the local superintendent. For example, the decision to establish an instructional materials facility or to inaugurate vocational education for the school district must be made by the board of education. But decisions about what in-

15

structional materials to include in the center or what kind of vocational curriculum is needed are decisions that should be made by the professional staff.

RECOMMENDATION 2 *The federal government should provide the types of assistance needed to improve local and state systems of education. Two types of federal assistance should be stressed: (a) the federal government should provide general financial assistance for the improvement of public education; (b) the U.S. Office of Education should have an expanded role in stimulating experimentation and innovation in the schools, in providing statistical analyses of importance, and in disseminating information about educational problems and promising practices.*

Federal government

The tradition of federal participation in education is almost as old as the nation itself, and it has been rapidly and greatly strengthened. Federal participation began with the Ordinance of 1785. Continuing through the Smith-Hughes Act of 1917 and other support for vocational education to the recent National Defense Education Act, the thrust of federal participation in public education has grown in breadth and strength. The impact of cooperatively set standards on vocational education curricula and the influence of the NDEA demonstrate the nature of the very real controls that have developed as a result of federal support for particular programs. They also indicate the kinds of program changes that can result when federal financial support is available.

The federal government is and should be a partner in the field of public education, taking its appropriate part along with localities and states. Its participation is inevitable because of the importance of education to the nation and because of its tax-collecting power. The range of activities of a strong federal educational agency should include:

16

- a wide variety of consultative services to state and local school systems for the improvement of educational programs
- increased distribution of information about promising curriculum practices
- stimulation and coordination of research, experimentation, and innovation in schools across the nation
- an expanded program of national conferences at which instructional leaders of state and local school systems, academic scholars, scholars in the profession of teaching, and leaders of education-related civic groups consider particular curriculum problems

Federal participation in the financial support of education has strengthened and can strengthen the public schools enormously, but it must follow appropriate principles. Federal financial support for the schools should take the form of general funds, rather than special-aid measures, and should be allocated to and administered by the states so that impoverished states can still offer education equal to the best in the country. The preference of Congress, however, is for specific educational programs that have clearly defined objectives and clearly defined limitations. When, and to what extent, Congress can be persuaded to move toward a general fund approach remains to be seen.

Local school faculties

RECOMMENDATION 3 *Local school faculties should have the freedom and the authority to make decisions about what to teach—within state and local requirements—and how to teach. Final instructional decisions should be made by the teacher, taking into consideration recommendations from appropriate local, state, and national groups representing the teaching profession, academic scholars, and the public.*

The teacher's decisions about daily classroom instruction determine the program that is offered to students. Wise decisions can make the school day a challenging adventure rather than a   17 routine chore or a tolerable interlude, and such decisions require sensitivity and intimate awareness of teachers. They should be made by the teacher or teachers responsible for a particular group of learners.

The range of effectiveness in making daily instructional decisions is great. Some teachers exert extraordinary creativeness, despite the frequency with which teaching decisions must be made and the limited amount of time available for planning. Others are more limited in their ability to make good decisions. But the right to independence in making teaching decisions, within the framework of existing societal and institutional plans, must not be taken away, even from teachers who make these decisions badly. Teachers who consistently make poor instructional decisions should be removed from teaching. It is the right to teach, not the right to make teaching decisions while employed as a teacher, that should be subject to impeachment.

State educational authorities

RECOMMENDATION 4 *State educational authorities should establish standards for public school instruction, provide adequate resources for their achievement, and give dynamic leadership to curriculum development, experimentation, and innovation in local schools.*

The state educational authority, by establishing standards and providing leadership for the improvement of local instructional programs, can lift the schools of every community from the potential limitations of provincialism and mediocrity. The state authority can make certain that the educational interests of the national community are served.

State education officials should use their resources and powers to encourage sound and active programs of curriculum study, experimentation, and innovation by local schools. Detailed curriculum prescriptions that are set forth and enforced by the state education department leave little room for creative development of local initiative.

State leadership should be exercised through procedures that have proved effective for stimulating improved instructional programs in local schools. Examples of such procedures include:

1. establishing a separate unit within the department specifically geared to stimulate and to finance the design and evaluation of new instructional programs in schools all across a state
2. providing coordination and some subsidy for the demonstration of new instructional programs
3. publishing curriculum materials that have been developed by statewide groups with membership including classroom teachers, school administrators, university professors from education and from the academic disciplines, and, when appropriate, lay citizens
4. sponsoring statewide or regional workshops and study conferences focused on particular curriculum problems, with membership from the groups listed just above
5. providing up-to-date and usable statistics and helping local units to do likewise
6. providing local school personnel with information about evaluations of available learning materials, proposals from national projects, and outstanding curriculum materials from other states

The state educational authority should stimulate curriculum experimentation and innovation through grants of funds, through collection and dissemination of information about results of experimentation, and sponsorship of cooperative projects involving colleges and universities, local school systems, and state education personnel. The state educational authority may also take the lead in evaluating curriculum proposals from special curriculum projects and national study groups. For example, individual states might establish their own curriculum evaluation commissions, or join with nearby states to set up such commissions to review and evaluate current curricular research and study.

The staff of the state educational authority should consist of personnel well prepared in curriculum and instruction, and in the subject matter fields, who are capable of providing statewide leadership. Political considerations should play no part in the   19 selection of members of the state's professional staff. There is great variation from state to state in the number and quality of such specialists on the professional staff, and this variation is reflected in the amount and effectiveness of the state's leadership for curriculum improvement. Local school systems, especially the smaller ones, need the help that can be provided by a strong professional staff at the state level.

RECOMMENDATION 5   *State legislatures should set forth general goals for the schools, provide adequate financial support, and delegate broad powers*
State *of implementation to the state and local educa-*
legislatures *tional authorities. The state legislature should* not *prescribe curriculum content or legislate specific courses.*

Lay control of educational policies determined by the legislative and executive branches of the state government is one matter, and the implementation of those policies by the professional staff of educators with the leadership of the chief state school officer is another. This distinction must be understood and respected if the maximum potential of all persons involved is to be realized. The state legislature is fulfilling its educational responsibilities when it enacts legislation describing general goals for the public schools, provides adequately for school support, and delegates broad powers of implementation to the staff of the state educational authority and to local school systems.

The National Committee for the Project on Instruction strongly opposes the tendency of a few legislatures to pass laws specifying course content and specific course objectives. The state legislature hampers effective education if it legislates a specific pattern of curriculum organization, assigns school time to various subjects, and sets forth a multitude of special educational requirements.

These problems of instructional decisions cannot be resolved by treatment in either-or terms. The question is not one of local or state or national control. It concerns, rather, the part that educational authorities at each level of government can most effectively take in the decision-making process, and the role that professional groups and other nationally oriented nongovernmental groups should take. The goal is to improve the program of instruction for young people by drawing on all our resources. The best approach is a partnership of all who are involved.

DECISION AREA II   Research, Experimentation, and Innovation

How can an extensive program of educational research, experimentation, and innovation be developed?

Improvement of the instructional program demands a climate favorable to change. It also demands resources—time, money, personnel—to support research and innovation.

Financial support for research and experimentation is negligible and belies the nation's professed devotion to education. Parents and politicians talk about the values of education, say they want high-quality instructional programs, and criticize the status quo. But often they make no connection between what they want from education and the path to its accomplishment. Professed beliefs in the values of education sound off key against the familiar background music of defeated bond issues, slashed budgets, watered-down measures for state and federal support and continuously increasing budgets for research and development in industry.

Private foundations contribute more and more to the support of research and innovation in education, but the general level of public support throughout the country is embarrassingly low. The "shoestring" approach to educational experimentation and research is, literally, ridiculous. Education in this country does not by any means live up to its potential. Nor will it even begin to until both the laudatory comments about the values of education and the often-justified criticisms of current practice are translated into the support needed to make a substantial differ-   21 ence in public education through strong, continuing, and wide-spread research and development programs.

RECOMMENDATION 6 *School systems should allocate an appropriate proportion of their annual operating budgets—not less than 1 per cent— for the support of research, experimentation, and innovation.*

Money, time, and personnel

Adequate time should be provided for each staff member to participate in curriculum planning, research, evaluation, and other activities designed to improve the instructional program.

In local school systems and in colleges and universities, highly competent people are needed to plan, conduct, and evaluate programs of educational change. Funds are needed to pay their salaries and to support the programs that are developed.

Teachers need time within the regular school schedule to participate in curriculum planning, research, evaluation, and other activities to improve the instructional program. A thought-provoking, creative approach to difficult instructional problems is not something to be undertaken by a half dozen tired teachers at four o'clock on Friday afternoon, however dedicated the teachers may be. It should be possible for members of a school staff to spend part of their regular working hours on such activities. Local communities can register their support of carefully designed research and experimentation by allocating time and a portion of the school budget—at least 1 per cent—for such educational activities.

RECOMMENDATION 7 *Adequately staffed and supported regional curriculum and instruction centers should be encouraged. These centers, located mainly in universities, should work in partnership with local schools to initiate innovation and conduct experimentation and research to improve the instructional program of the public schools.*

Regional curriculum and instruction centers

Regional curriculum and instruction centers can make major contributions to educational reform. These centers should be staffed with persons who understand the theory and practice of curriculum and instruction; in addition, the centers should have access to specialists in the behavioral sciences and the academic disciplines. All inquiry should be independent. For these reasons, it is recommended that the centers be located in major universities possessing the necessary resources.

The centers should not operate degree-granting programs, although many members of the staffs should be members of university departments in which courses and seminars for degrees are offered. The centers most certainly should provide a wide range of refresher clinics and mid-career institutes for teachers, supervisors, curriculum directors, and administrators.

Any school system seeking to bring its staff members up to date in their respective fields could send able personnel to these centers. School districts would participate in the financial costs of maintaining the centers. In return, the schools would benefit by consultant help from a large field staff and by the upgrading of their own personnel.

At the outset, each center might select an area of emphasis and also plan to cooperate on the emphases selected by other centers. For example, one center might develop alternative curriculum designs. Local schools could study these designs and adapt them to their needs. A second center might, at regular intervals, collect and evaluate data showing the status of curriculum and instruction in the public schools. A third center might emphasize experimentation in curriculum sequences, seeking to determine appropriate timing and pacing for introducing learnings and aiding the progress of learners of varying abilities. A fourth might study patterns of curriculum decision-making at local, state, and national levels. A fifth might develop techniques for appraising instructional materials and pass on these techniques to professional groups engaged in selecting learning resources.

Such centers would provide unique opportunities for the cooperative participation and mutual advantage of federal, state, and local government agencies. For example, a center experimenting with curricular sequences for learners of varied abilities could help state departments of education to use more than guesswork in providing funds for teaching various subject fields. School districts trying to upgrade their instructional programs could secure assistance from these centers in changing teaching procedures with considerable assurance that they would improve children's learning. Local school boards confronted by pressure to ban certain instructional materials or to install others could draw upon expert analyses carried on in an impartial setting.

Curriculum and instruction centers could, in an organized fashion, bring greater understanding about public education to the general public through such activities as seminar series on specific topics, establishment of speakers' bureaus, or maintenance of strong programs of information.

University centers for inquiry, experimentation, and research into the substantive and political aspects of curriculum planning could alleviate much lay and professional uncertainty about substantive curriculum problems. They could also contribute to better understanding and better use of sound processes in curriculum planning.

RECOMMENDATION 8 *Efforts of nationally oriented, nongovernmental groups to stimulate curricular `and instructional experimentation and innovation should be encouraged. Scholars in the academic fields and the teaching profession should be involved in such efforts.*

*Nongovern-
mental
groups*

National commissions and committees sponsored by professional educational organizations or other groups can profitably make studies and recommendations on all aspects of the instructional program. The support of private foundations is increasing the number of adequately financed projects aimed at the improvement of education, particularly through the encouragement of experimentation and innovation.

24   The growing number of special subject-area studies and other

programs point to the need for more national leadership. Non-governmental commissions working on programs of a national scale can be expected to be sensitive to the need for balance between the national and the local interest and also to strive for balance among the various parts of the curriculum.

These programs are intended, finally, for the school classroom. It would be well, therefore, for the teaching profession to take a vigorous and positive role in both developing and evaluating these studies so that the particular experience and viewpoint of the profession can be utilized.

SUMMARY

The answers to complex educational problems are not to be found at the back of any book. The answers—the good ones—develop from painstaking attention to the kinds of questions that focus thought and action on significant and pertinent decisions. Even as educators are arriving at decisions on the issues of a given period, the guidelines are changing. Only by a continuing quest for knowledge and awareness of all the shifts and changes that occur in the determining conditions of education can its leaders hope to be responsive to the needs of the individual and society.

Some of the determining conditions have been reviewed in this chapter, and two of the questions the Committee believes to be the right questions for this period in our history have been discussed. "Who should make what decisions about education?" "How can an extensive program of educational research, experimentation, and innovation be developed?" Some suggested answers to these questions are contained in the eight recommendations included in this chapter.

Seven questions that focus attention on decisions about what to teach are considered in the chapter that follows.

For a more detailed discussion of the material in Chapter 2, the reader is referred to the supporting Project volume, Deciding What to Teach. *Dorothy M. Fraser was the principal writer of that report.*

◦⧓◦

Chapter 2

DECIDING
WHAT TO
TEACH

"What shall the schools teach?"

This is a continuing question, one to which each generation must find its own answer, drawing upon the past for what is still appropriate, and making changes to reflect the needs, hopes, values, and possibilities of its own day.

Within the lifetime of our own country, the question of what the schools should teach has been answered in different ways at different times. For example, the classical curriculum of the colonial Latin grammar school gave way to the broader program of the nineteenth-century secondary school. This, in turn, was revolutionized in the twentieth century as the high school became an instrument of education for all youth instead of a single-purpose, college preparatory institution. In the elementary school, as in the high school, the program has changed as different answers have been given to the question of what to teach. Subject areas have increased in number and variety; content once reserved for the secondary school has been dropped into the elementary school; curriculum content once reserved for the college has found its way into the high school.

Today, as for many generations, the question of what the schools should teach continues to be debated and to bring forth different answers from different people. In this chapter, the National Committee for the NEA Project on Instruction identifies seven decision areas, makes eleven recommendations related to the decisions, and summarizes the reasoning behind each recommendation.

DECISION AREA III   Educating All Children and Youth

How can the instructional program of the school be designed to develop the individual potentialities of all members of the school population within the framework of a society that values both unity and diversity?

This question takes into account the following ideas about the United States and its people:

• The people of this country have committed themselves to the proposition that all children and youth in the United States shall be educated. Ideally, this commits us to developing the potentialities of all members of the school population. Because of economic imbalances and racial strife, equal educational opportunity is sadly lacking for many children and youth. Hopefully, this generation of Americans will come closer to the realization of this goal.

• Differences among and within individuals make it necessary to differentiate the instructional program in order to achieve educational goals. These differences also help to provide the diversity valued in our culture.

• Unity within the nation is strengthened by a common background of knowledge, skills, and values. Part of this background can be provided through the schools.

RECOMMENDATION 9   *The instructional program should provide: (a) opportunities for developing the individual potentialities represented in the wide range of differences among people; (b) a common fund of knowledge, values, and skills vital to the welfare of the individual and the nation.*

The individual and the nation

To achieve these objectives, the instructional program cannot be the same for all. Provision for individual differences should be made by qualified teaching personnel through diagnosis of learning needs and through appropriate variety of content, resources for learning, and instructional methods.

In a society that values both unity and diversity, the school is called upon to help establish bases for unity and to provide opportunities for developing the unique potentialities of the individual. Our millions of people, diverse though they are and should be, find strength and personal satisfaction in the unity that comes from a common background. Though there are wide varieties of opinion and of cultures represented in these United States, the freedom with which differences and disagreements are aired among disparate groups sometimes obscures but does not diminish common ties. Americans stand together when a demagogue threatens the freedoms they have learned to respect and have sacrificed to defend. How, indeed, can they safeguard these liberties and protect the right of the individual to be different, unless they share with each other a firm commitment to these ideals—a commitment rooted in a common background of knowledge and values?

But the need for a common background cannot be met through a uniform program of instruction; neither can the need for developing the unique potentialities of each individual. The public schools serve forty million individuals in the elementary and secondary schools, each individual with his own pattern of potentialities and problems. Some of the forty million learn quickly in certain fields and slowly in others; some are consistently rapid, average, or slow in most fields of study. Some have clear-cut realistic standards and goals toward which they strive effectively; others have goals that are unrealistically high; still others drift without definite aim.

Students come with differing expectations about what education has to offer them and about the length of time they will remain in school. At one extreme are those who wait impatiently for the birthday that legally frees them from school; at the other extreme are those who look forward eagerly to college and a professional education.

In short, students in our public schools represent a cross section of the abilities and aspirations of the nation. Obviously, the educational needs of all these young people cannot be met by a uniform program of instruction. Nor can the needs of our country be met by such a program. Those who advocate a uniform program for all ignore both the unique nature of each individual and the diversified nature of American life. Equal educational opportunity for all, yes. The same program for all, no. A common body of knowledge, values, and skills, yes. One way of teaching them, no.

DECISION AREA IV   Establishing Priorities for the School

What are the distinctive responsibilities of the school in contrast to those that are distinctive to the family, the church, industry, and various youth-serving agencies?

What responsibilities should the school share with other institutions and with other youth-serving agencies?

What, then, should be included in the school program?

What should be excluded from it?

The question, "What shall the schools teach?" and its counterpart, "What shall the schools *not* teach?" constitute a central issue in attempts to appraise American education. Stated in behavioral terms, the questions then become, "What should the graduate be able to do that he could not do if he had not gone to school?"

At a general level, there is agreement. Laymen and educators alike agree that the school has a major responsibility for preparing young people to live in today's society. They agree that the school has a responsibility for preparing young people to live with change and contribute to constructive change. At a more specific level, they agree that the student should read, write, speak, compute, and think more effectively than he would had he not gone to school.

Great differences of opinion appear, however, when educators and laymen, together or separately, approach the more complex tasks that come next:

- deciding what knowledge, what skills, what values are needed by children and young people
- determining what knowledge, what skills, what values can best be taught by the school; what knowledge, skills, and values can best be taught by the home, the church, and other social institutions
- deciding which learnings require the joint efforts of the school and other agencies

The differences in opinion are reflected in widely varying recommendations as to what should be given major treatment in the schools, what should receive only peripheral attention, and what should be excluded altogether. Some people favor an expanded school program with a broad range of subjects, both practical and academic. Others prefer a restricted program focused sharply on academic subjects.

Some people question the school's concern for the social development of the child and for his physical and mental health. They say, in effect: "These responsibilities belong to the home and the church. When the school tries to take them on, it usurps the prerogatives of other institutions and abdicates its own major responsibility, the intellectual development of young people."

Others reply: "There is a difference between what ought to be and what is. The physical and mental health needs of many children are not being met by the family or any other agency. If a student has difficulties with health or with emotional adjustment, the school can make little progress in encouraging his intellectual development until these problems are solved—through the school if no other institution accepts responsibility." On this particular debate, most educators believe that health *services* are a shared responsibility of the schools. However, the content of health *instruction* belongs in the school curriculum because such knowledge is necessary, is most efficiently learned in school, and no other public agency provides such instruction.

31

All of these opinions reflect different ideas about the proper role of the school in American society. Equally great differences appear when efforts are made to define the responsibilities of other youth-serving agencies in relationship to the school program. Resulting difficulties in making decisions about what the schools should teach must be faced and resolved. The education of a child is not confined to his experiences in school; family, church, mass media, nonschool recreational facilities, and social agencies in the community are powerful educational forces. Their complex relationships to the schooling of young people should be studied carefully when efforts are made to establish priorities for the instructional program of the schools.

Distinctive and shared responsibilities

RECOMMENDATION 10   *Priorities for the school are the teaching of skills in reading, composition, listening, speaking (both native and foreign languages), and computation ... ways of creative and disciplined thinking, including methods of inquiry and application of knowledge ... competence in self-instruction and independent learning ... fundamental understanding of the humanities and the arts, the social sciences and the natural sciences, and mathematics ... appreciation of and discriminating taste in literature, music, and the visual arts ... instruction in health education and physical education.*

Responsibilities best met by joint efforts of the school and other social agencies include: development of values and ideals ... social and civic competence ... vocational preparation.

The decision to include or exclude particular school subjects or outside-of-class activities should be based on: (a) the priorities assigned to the school and to other agencies; (b) data about learners and society, and developments in the academic disciplines; (c) the human and material resources available in the school and community.

In the United States, the school is society's chief agent for systematically inducting each new generation into its culture. The distinctive responsibilities of the school grow out of this role. To determine specifically just what these distinctive responsibilities are, it is important to find answers to the questions implied in the three tasks cited on page 31. These questions are:

- What knowledge, values, and skills do children and youth in our culture need to learn?
- Which of these goals can best be achieved by the school?
- What knowledge, skills, and values can best be taught by the home, the church, and other social institutions?
- Which learnings require the joint efforts of the school and other agencies?

Thoughtful consideration of these questions is needed to determine priorities for the schools—to make sure, for example, that reading is identified as more important than cheerleading. Those responsible for deciding what to teach should apply concrete standards just as the purchaser of an automobile applies certain criteria in deciding which car to buy. (Styling has highest priority; gasoline mileage ranks fifth.) Suppose, for example, that there are pressures for adding French, German, or Norwegian to the curriculum of the third grade, or for pushing physics and geometry down into the first grade. The problem might be approached in three ways.

First, assume the school should do what the current pressure indicates and add these subjects. The result is the "creeping" curriculum: "Never have so many learned so little about so much." A second way to approach this problem is to say, "Fine! We will add these subjects if you will tell us what subjects to remove from the curriculum."

A third approach to the problem of what the school ought properly to provide requires that educators and the public apply suitable criteria. The following questions might be considered with reference to an area of learning proposed for inclusion in the instructional program:[7]

1. Is it learning that is based substantially upon bodies of organized knowledge, such as the arts and sciences?

2. Is it learning of complex and difficult things that requires organization of experience and distribution of practice over long periods of time?

3. Is it learning in which the essential factors must be brought specially to the attention of the learner? For example, concepts that explain the growth of plants are not obvious to an observer of plants.

4. Is it an experience that cannot be provided directly in the ordinary activities of daily living?

5. Is it learning that requires a more structured experience than is usually available in life outside the school?

6. Is it learning that requires re-examination and interpretation of experience?

Whatever priorities are assigned to the school, it should be clear that an area of instruction which is high on the priority list is not, therefore, off limits to all other youth-serving agencies. To say, for example, that the teaching of reading is a priority for the school is not to imply that the school is the sole teacher of reading. The school enlists the support of the family, finds ways to use the mass media of communication, works with the public library to expand reading interests and skills. To identify the teaching of reading as a major responsibility of the school is to say: (1) reading is a skill needed by all children and youth; (2) it can be learned efficiently by most children only through systematic instruction; and (3) no other public agency, accessible to all children and youth, provides such systematic instruction.

The development of values, civic and social competence, and preparation for a vocation require the joint efforts of the school and other agencies. The school, therefore, has obligations in these important areas, but its obligations are modified by the fact that other agencies share the responsibilities. How much the school's obligations are modified, and in what ways, depend in part on the needs and resources of the local community.

Decisions about the school program—what to include, what to exclude, and what to emphasize—should be made by the local school system. They should be made within the framework of state requirements and with due attention to both distinctive and shared responsibilities. The relative emphasis on distinctive and shared areas of learning may vary considerably from school to school. It *should* vary according to the socioeconomic backgrounds of students and the services available to them from other institutions and agencies. For example, a good school in a slum neighborhood would provide means for all students to develop a basic core of knowledge, values, and skills, but it could wisely emphasize cultural and work opportunities which might otherwise be unavailable to the pupils.

In some communities nonschool agencies have steadily increased the services provided for young people. Some of these services may duplicate efforts of the school. If student needs in some areas are adequately met by other agencies and institutions, the school should restrict its activities in these areas and apply its resources to the functions which are peculiarly its own. Nevertheless, the school cannot abdicate its share of responsibility for seeing that the total range of the educational needs of youth are well served, either by the school or by nonschool agencies. To this end, the school should encourage the coordination of activities of all youth-serving agencies. It should also stimulate the development of services that are needed but not available—services that the school cannot, and perhaps should not, provide from its own resources.

DECISION AREA V   The School's Role in Dealing with National Problems Related to Youth

What is the school's role in dealing with serious national problems such as youth unemployment and juvenile delinquency?

The schools' role is easy to define in words and incredibly difficult to play when the actors are real-life characters. The role of the school is to provide a program that makes sense to the total school population, that challenges and persuades all children and youth to remain in school because something recognizably valuable is being provided. Fulfillment of this role is important for the sake of the young people themselves and vital to the survival of our society.

In a society as complex and fast paced as ours, it will be the rare individual who can master without some formal education the skills he needs in order to be self-supporting, self-respecting, and self-directing. The schools are challenged to make the most of whatever amount of time a student spends in them. They are particularly challenged to develop programs that will keep young people in school beyond the compulsory attendance age.

This puts a heavy responsibility on the elementary school, and rightly so. The child who finds satisfaction and recognizable values in his first school experiences is likely, as an adolescent and youth, to feel that further schooling will also be rewarding. He will give the high school a chance. But if the high school disappoints him, and if there is no adult pressure to keep him in school, he may become a dropout. If his experiences in the elementary school are unsatisfactory, he enters high school only if he has to, and he may drop out as soon as the laws of his state permit.

The dropout problem is not new, but it is in many ways more serious than it once was. Certainly it is more closely related to unemployment. Many young people who quit school thirty years ago dropped out of schools that, regrettably, were not challenging. But they "dropped into" a society that had a place for them. At that time, roughly 40 per cent of the labor force were in the unskilled or semiskilled category. Today there is a rapidly increasing demand for high-level skills and a rapidly decreasing demand for unskilled labor. The rate of unemployment, now, among school dropouts who are sixteen to twenty-one years of age almost never falls below 20 per cent; in the slum areas of the big cities it is sometimes as high as 70 per cent. The dropout problem also relates to juvenile delinquency. Most dropouts are not delinquent, but the rate of delinquency among dropouts is nine to twelve times higher than it is among those who stay in school.

The problems of youth unemployment and juvenile delinquency are especially persistent problems among the economically and culturally deprived. Today, the intensified migration to urban areas points up the fact that there are literally millions of citizens who, in our culture, are disadvantaged. They are people whose low incomes are associated with poor housing; overcrowding; inadequate attention to physical well-being; limited or uncertain access to books, theaters, concerts, libraries, museums; limited access to the kinds of educational programs that would be most useful to them or their children.

The nation's fourteen largest cities have a steadily increasing number of culturally deprived young people. In 1950, one child out of every four in these cities was culturally deprived. In 1960, the figure was one in three. By 1970, there will be one deprived child for every two. Actually, this ratio already exists in four of these fourteen cities.

If the schools cannot reach these young people with programs that are meaningful and that identify and develop the talent which is there to be developed, the loss to individuals and to society will be tragic and costly. Part of the school's role in helping to combat such problems as juvenile delinquency relates to the development of instructional programs geared to the needs of this large segment of the population.

The National Committee for the Project on Instruction makes the following recommendation.

Youth unemployment and juvenile delinquency

RECOMMENDATION 11   *The schools can help to combat such serious national problems as youth unemployment and juvenile delinquency by: (a) evaluating the intellectual and creative potential of all children and youth in the schools; (b) identifying early the potential dropout and delinquent; (c) developing positive programs to challenge these young people to educational endeavor; (d) participating in cooperative programs with parents and with community groups and organizations— business and industry, labor, service groups, government agencies, and the many youth-serving agencies.*

37

A school staff that faces its instructional problems realistically will find much valuable help in the growing body of information about children and youth in today's society, particularly about urban children and youth. Current studies in sociology, psychology, and education yield information about factors that frequently deter learning and about ways in which schools can cope with these factors. The studies challenge some of the assumptions and point out some of the misconceptions that have stood in the way of educating children who are economically and culturally deprived.

One misconception has to do with the intellectual capacities of these young people. Much work has been done, and much more needs to be done, to devise techniques that provide accurate information about the intellectual and creative capacities of people from *all* kinds of backgrounds, and particularly those from economically and culturally deprived groups. Most of the commonly used standardized tests of intelligence and achievement are inappropriate for these young people, and the evidence they yield is not reliable.

Because inappropriate or unreliable measuring instruments are used, many children and youth from culturally disadvantaged backgrounds are unfairly labeled. As a result, they are misunderstood, mistaught, and misdirected. Their unrecognized intelligence is assaulted but not dented by an instructional program that has little relationship to their unique needs or their real potentials. Bored with the whole process of schooling, many young people mark time until the day they can remove themselves physically from the school they long ago deserted psychologically. To their credit, some of these misjudged youth stubbornly refuse to accept the label that is placed upon them. Too often, however, the label is just about what their earlier experiences have taught them to expect. It is accepted, and this acceptance in itself effectively blocks the effort to learn—sometimes permanently.

Another assumption is that a large number of children who are economically and culturally deprived—in particular, the potential dropouts—are not interested in education. This assumption rests heavily, but precariously, on the fact that many of these young people are discontented with school. They are discontented with school, but they are not necessarily disinterested in education. In their experience and in their vocabulary, "school" and "education" are not always synonymous.

Recommendation 11 also suggests the need for identifying the potential dropout and potential delinquent. Increasing attention is being given to dropouts, and current studies yield much information that is useful for teachers and curriculum planners.

Whatever their intelligence and rate of learning, the young people who drop out of school at an early age share one characteristic: a school record of difficulty and failure. The implication seems to be fairly obvious—identify potential dropouts. More important, identify the points at which the school is failing these young people and the reasons why. Exercise initiative in developing programs more likely to meet the needs of these students. Explore the increasing number of experimental programs and try out the practices that seem most promising and most appropriate. Work with community groups and organizations that are helping, or can help, with the solution of some of the problems.

Experimental programs are under way in various places throughout the country. Some of them are in rural areas; more are in urban areas. They are concerned with an age-school range beginning with prekindergarten and continuing through the high school. Some of the current studies and experiments are described in *Deciding What To Teach*. Included among them is the Project on School Dropouts,[8] a program being carried on by the National Education Association.

So much attention has been given the school and community dropout problems of large cities that the need to strengthen rural schools has been overshadowed. Many of the school difficulties of rural migrants to these cities—Washington and Chicago, for example—have been aggravated by poor preparation. This is often, but not always, the result of segregation. Mountain areas of Kentucky and Tennessee need help for their schools.

The problems of the dropout, the unemployed youth, and the juvenile delinquent are serious ones for both the individual and society. But the attacks that are being made on the problems are vigorous and constructive and the results are encouraging. In literature that is developing from current studies and experiments, there is a vitality and an optimism that should be reassuring and challenging to young people and to their teachers.

What is the school's role in teaching about controversial issues and about communism and other ideologies?

The view that controversial issues should be studied in school by American youth has widespread but not unanimous approval. The National Committee for the Project on Instruction believes that such issues should be included in both the elementary and secondary school curriculum.

Students, like their parents and teachers, live in the midst of controversy over many issues. Differences of opinion are a continuing and important part of life in a democratic society; they are to be respected, encouraged, resolved. It is, therefore, a responsibility of the school to help young people develop the skills of rational thought that are needed for an objective approach to a study of issues on which men differ.

Controversial issues

RECOMMENDATION 12   *Rational discussion of controversial issues should be an important part of the school program. The teacher should help students identify relevant information, learn the techniques of critical analysis, make independent judgments, and be prepared to present and support them. The teacher should also help students become sensitive to the continuing need for objective re-examination of issues in the light of new information and changing conditions in society.*

40

The emphasis in study about controversial issues should be on learning how to understand significant unsolved problems of society and to arrive at rational conclusions about them. The skills that are needed are those that will serve the individual throughout a lifetime of association with controversy. Ideas must be examined, assumptions explored, information gathered and evaluated for its relevance and relative significance. In the study of an issue there should be respect for divergent ideas and for the individuals who hold them.

One point of view is that the teacher is not a neutral observer in this total process—objective, yes, but not neutral. Brackenbury says:[9]

> Impotency, not impartiality, is achieved by the teacher who keeps his own convictions hidden. The teacher who presents all sides of a controversial issue and then says, 'Now, children, make up your own minds where you stand,' is perhaps nobly motivated. But he is sadly misguided. Can his students be blamed for concluding that perhaps it does not make any difference which side they take or whether they take any side at all? Somehow their teacher seems to manage without taking a stand on any significant issue. If he makes a virtue out of keeping his thoughts hidden, he can hardly condemn his students for wondering what he thinks or whether thinking really matters at all.

Good judgment should be exercised in the selection of controversial issues to be studied. The following criteria provide some guides for deciding whether or not a particular topic warrants consideration in the classroom.

1. Is the issue suitable for pupils of the maturity and backgrounds represented in the group?

One test of the appropriateness of an issue for study is whether or not it can be made significant to students. One clue is interest; students themselves identify topics that concern them. For certain age groups, proposals for solving problems of juvenile delinquency or for lowering the voting age are immediately interesting. The treatment of controversial issues should not, however, be limited to those which students happen to bring up. It is 41 a responsibility of the teacher to stimulate interest in topics which can be made significant to students as well as to be sensitive to those which require too much artificial respiration. However, the teacher should avoid assuming prematurely that a given issue cannot be made significant to young people. The broad issue may be too complex, but there may be a particular aspect that young people can study with profit.

2. Is the issue one for which adequate resources, human and material, are available?

A wide variety of instructional materials should be accessible to students and should include presentations of differing viewpoints. The identification of appropriate resources is a task to be undertaken by both students and teachers and extends far beyond the location of printed materials in the school library. It should, in fact, begin with a consideration of the many possible sources from which relevant information might be gathered. The early conclusion that adequate resources are not available may point to lack of imagination and judgment in identifying the people, the films, the newspapers, the TV programs, the visits to civic centers, the infinite variety of sources from which relevant data may be gathered.

The teacher is, of course, one of the resources and should be prepared to make appropriate contributions to the exploration of the particular topics being studied. This does not mean that the teacher is an expert in every issue, nor that he necessarily contributes most by expounding on an issue from the vantage point of his own information. Good teaching is not "telling." It is the art of helping others acquire skills needed for present and future learnings. Adequate preparation for guiding learning about a particular topic may mean knowing the pertinent resources and making them accessible to students.

3. Is the issue one which is important and likely to be of continuing significance?

Since a reasonably full study of a few issues will be more valuable than brief study of many, a selection should be made among those that meet the foregoing criteria. Just as some historical or scientific facts are more important than others and therefore are more worth studying, so some controversial issues are more significant than others and deserve priority. Also, a problem that promises to be of continuing importance is more significant to study than one which is ephemeral in nature.

Current
social forces
and trends

RECOMMENDATION 13 *To help the student think critically about current issues, the curriculum should provide opportunities for adequate instruction concerning social forces and trends. Attention commensurate with their significance in modern society should be given to issues such as international relations, economic growth, urbanization, population growth, science and technology, and mass media.*

Educating students to be effective in their culture includes acquainting them with outstanding social forces and emerging trends. It includes helping youth learn to apply rational analysis and critical thinking to contemporary social problems. No one expects that students will "solve" the problems they study in the sense that "solving" requires definitive action. But through study, young people can gain better understanding of the issues of this decade and be better prepared to cope intelligently with critical problems of the future. The problems of tomorrow will be related to social forces and trends of today. Youth cannot be given a blueprint of their adult world, with specific descriptions of its achievements and tensions, but they can develop a background of information to help them understand new problems as they emerge. And they can acquire skill in analyzing current forces and predicting the future direction of social change.

Identifying social trends is a matter of predicting from available evidence. As evidence is augmented, the prediction may be reinforced or modified. The study of social trends should be based on factual information. It should give sufficient attention   43 to the methods of analysis used by scholars for young people to understand how conclusions are derived and to realize that current conclusions are likely to be modified in the future.

RECOMMENDATION 14   *The school curriculum should include a study of political and social ideologies, focusing upon communism. The methods of rational inquiry should be stressed. The study should be set in the perspective of the modern world and be incorporated into the instructional program at appropriate points. If a special unit on communism is deemed desirable in the secondary school, it should supplement and complement earlier study of these topics.*

Teaching about communism

As with other areas of the curriculum, decisions about what to teach *and* how to teach *about these topics should be based upon policies developed by school administrators and teachers of the local school system. In the formulation and implementation of such policies, school personnel should utilize the resources of scholarship and be supported in their decisions by the school board and by an informed community opinion.*

Students should be encouraged to be objective in their study. They should explore the strengths and accomplishments as well as the weaknesses and failures of various kinds of societies, including modern communistic societies. The senior high school should teach about communism when it is appropriate in the study of history, American problems, and economics. Constitutional democracy, capitalism, democratic socialism, and the various forms of totalitarian government should be included. Present-day communism should be regarded as a specific historical movement related to economic factors as well as to political history in the parts of the world where it prevails.

The more intensive study of communism may well be delayed until the senior high school, but the topic should receive appropriate attention in the elementary school. The young child is no stranger to such words as "communist," "Red," "Khrushchev," and "sputnik." He has his own ideas about communism—ideas picked up from a hodgepodge of juvenile and adult conversation, comic strips, radio programs, television shows, newspapers, and magazines. He has questions and fears generated by what he has seen and heard. The elementary school teacher who understands basic facts about communism can help the child answer some questions, verify some conclusions, and clarify some inaccurate ideas. Furthermore, as the climate for teaching about communism becomes more favorable, producers of textbooks and audio-visual materials will respond with resources for learning geared to various levels of maturity.

Many excellent articles, booklets, books, and bibliographies are already available, but teachers often do not know about them. The major problem with materials is not *availability* but *accessibility*.

Some national organizations have developed reasonable and scholarly materials, but even at this level some extreme groups base their programs on emotion rather than on reason. Commendable statements and teaching aids have been developed by such organizations as the American Bar Association, the American Legion, the American Political Science Association, the Chamber of Commerce, the National Council for the Social Studies, and the National Education Association.

A program of teaching about communism and about international relations needs to provide teachers with opportunities for studying the economics, political science, and history that are essential to the task. This opportunity can be provided by universities and by other qualified professional agencies through in-service education.

The study of communism and other ideologies should do more than simply indoctrinate students on the good of democracy and the evils of communism. A black-and-white approach, by denying the very essence of the democratic way, defeats itself. Knowledge rests on established facts, and attitudes should result from an open, yet critical, mind. Wise teaching will add to the strength of American democratic traditions and thought.

DECISION AREA VII   A Balanced Program

How can the school provide a balanced program for the individual and maintain it amidst various pressures for specialization?

Consideration of this question requires that attention be given to such related questions as: What is a balanced program for the individual? What are the bases for good decisions about what constitutes a balanced program? How can the school maintain balance when there are strong pressures to increase the emphasis on certain aspects of the program? How can the school maintain balance when increased emphasis on one part of the curriculum results in decreased emphasis on some other part?

For these questions there is a brief, although not simple, answer—the school can clarify its educational goals and stand by them.

The major goal is the development of individuals who can fulfill their responsibilities to society and find personal satisfaction in creative and constructive activity—people who think clearly, feel deeply, and act wisely. To achieve this goal there is need for a program that provides balance: balance of content; balance between academic and applied subjects; balance among knowledge, values, and skills; balance between what the school provides and what is available through other social agencies; balance in variety and use of extraclass activities; balance of concern for the individual and for society. A balanced program for each student does not mean a uniform program for all. A balanced program for one person may be unbalanced for another, and vice versa.

The National Committee for the Project on Instruction makes the following recommendation for achieving and maintaining 46   balance in the instructional program.

RECOMMENDATION 15   *The school can provide and maintain a curriculum appropriately balanced for each student by offering a comprehensive program of studies, making early and continuous assessment of individual potentialities and achievements, and providing individualized programs based on careful counseling.*

Ways of achieving balance

To avoid the imbalance that can result from limiting financial support to certain selected subjects and services, general financial support should be provided for the total program. This applies to local, state, and federal support.

As indicated earlier, balance has many dimensions, each one deserving careful attention. The various aspects of balance are discussed in detail in *Deciding What To Teach*. One aspect, balance of content, is considered here.

Balance of content requires appropriate attention to the natural and physical sciences, mathematics, the social sciences, the humanities, and the applied subjects. Recently, there has been an unprecedented effort to improve the quality and increase the amount of instruction in science and mathematics, fields that have been relatively static in the school curriculum. This effort has been given impetus by Soviet achievements in space and by fear that United States leadership in science and technology is threatened. In the minds of many people, including members of the United States Congress, national survival seemed to be at stake. Since 1955, sizable allocations of federal funds have been provided for science and mathematics through the National Defense Education Act and the National Science Foundation. In addition, private foundations have supported major curriculum projects on various aspects of science and mathematics instruction in the public schools.

The teaching of modern foreign languages has also been given a priority, comparable to science and mathematics, on the premise that it, too, can contribute to "national survival." But with this exception, efforts to improve school programs in the social   47 sciences and the humanities have not made as much headway; support needed for experimentation in these fields has not, until recently, been available either from public or private sources.

One measure of the relative emphasis placed on the sciences, the social sciences, and the humanities in recent years is reflected in public support. In 1961, of the $969 million the federal government spent in support of basic research, 71 per cent went to the physical sciences; 26 per cent to the life sciences; 2 per cent to the psychological sciences; and 1 per cent to the social sciences. Virtually nothing went to research in the humanities.[10] Another measure may be found in the number of nationally oriented curriculum projects in each field. Early in 1962, a review of such projects revealed the following information: in science and mathematics, twenty-five projects were in progress or had recently been completed; in the social studies, seven were reported; in the English language arts, four; and in the arts, none.[11]

Early in 1963, however, the Ford Foundation announced the grant of nearly 1.4 million dollars to the Music Educators National Conference, a department of the NEA, for a six-year contemporary music project focused on creativity in the elementary and secondary schools.[12] In June 1963, a national Commission on the Humanities was established by the American Council of Learned Societies, the Council of Graduate Schools in the United States, and the United Chapters of Phi Beta Kappa to review the state of the humanities and to recommend means of improving their teaching, scholarship, and creativity. The National Committee for the Project on Instruction commends these efforts and anticipates that by the end of the decade much more attention will be directed to the humanities.

Health education is another area that deserves and is receiving foundation support. A four-year School Health Education Study aimed at improving instruction in this field is currently being conducted in cooperation with the American Association for Health, Physical Education, and Recreation and the NEA. This study is supported by a grant of over $300,000 from the Samuel Bronfman Foundation.

The recent emphasis on science and mathematics has helped to correct an imbalance that existed in the instructional program in the 1950s. But has a new imbalance been created, with the humanities and the social sciences being neglected at a time when their contributions are much needed? Science and mathematics are powerful servants of mankind, but they may not be its saviors. Those who solve peaceably the problems that harass nations and threaten humanity with destruction must understand economic, social, political, and human problems as well.

Furthermore, in our preoccupation with survival we can not lose sight of the prime question: "Survival for what?" Why survive if the resources that spell self-realization, health, and personal satisfaction are not to be explored? Why survive if the knowledge and skills that are needed for interested and intelligent participation in the world's economic, social, and political problems are not to be learned at a highly usable level?

In a society that is increasingly complex, standardized, and mechanized, the individual needs more help than ever before in achieving a sense of personal significance and self-realization and in acquiring an adequate knowledge of his society's problems. For the school this means providing an instructional program that includes materials drawn from the social sciences and the humanities as well as from the natural sciences. Curriculum experimentation and in-service study in these fields should be supported by state and local educational authorities. Hopefully, federal and private foundation support will also be available. But if such help is not forthcoming, then state and local educational authorities will have to give priority, in budget and program, to fields neglected by other sources of support.

DECISION AREA VIII   Selecting Content

How can schools make wise selections of content from the ever-growing body of available knowledge?

The amount of knowledge from which to choose is overpowering in its magnitude, and the rate at which advances are being made is so rapid that new developments confront us before old ones are fully understood. We can no longer see the topmost point on this mounting pile of knowledge. The top is somewhere far beyond our range of vision and rising, so we assume, toward outer space.

Never before have the dynamic forces of change spun with such incredible speed. In the nearly 2,000 years since the birth of Christ, there has been first a very slow and then a rapidly accelerating growth in the accumulation of knowledge. If this accumulation is plotted on a time line, beginning with the birth of Christ, it is estimated that the first doubling of knowledge occurred in 1750, the second in 1900, the third in 1950, and the fourth only ten years later, 1960!

So much has been learned in so many areas of knowledge that it is no longer possible for students to learn even summaries of existing knowledge. Sheer bulk defeats any effort to teach knowledge as a body of facts to be learned, Furthermore, we can expect radical reorganization of a given body of knowledge not once in the remainder of this century but several times. The school problem once known as "coverage" is meaningless and obsolete. Coverage is no longer difficult, it is impossible!

The problems of what to learn and how to learn it require a different approach today. We need to find ways to move from memorization of facts to discovery of facts, ways to help young students think as physicists think, as historians think, as artists think.

How, then, can schools make wise selections of content? How can they make intelligent use of the findings and methods of the disciplines? And, in the process, what are the appropriate roles of academic scholars, educators, and laymen? The National Committee for the Project on Instruction makes three recommendations.

RECOMMENDATION 16   *The objectives of the school, with a clear statement of priorities, should give direction to all curriculum planning. This* *Bases for* *applies to adding content, eliminating content, or* *selecting* *changing the emphases on various topics and fields* *content* *of study.*

50

Content earns its place in the curriculum by its contribution to the achievement of educational objectives. The establishment of objectives should, therefore, precede any effort to determine content of the instructional program and to determine relative emphases to be placed on various aspects of the program. Since the real purpose of education is to bring about desired changes in the behavior of students—changes in thinking, feeling and acting—statements of objectives should indicate precisely the specific kinds of behavior sought.

Obviously, the objectives themselves need reconsideration from time to time. But when they are valid and clear, and only then, educational objectives are dependable guides to good decisions about what is needed to achieve them.

Keeping content up-to-date

RECOMMENDATION 17 *Each curriculum area should be under continuous study and evaluation and should be reviewed periodically. One purpose of such reviews is to determine whether recent findings in the academic disciplines are, or should be, reflected in the instructional program. These reviews should utilize the knowledge and skills of the teacher, the school administrator, the scholar in the academic disciplines, the scholar in the profession of teaching, and the lay citizen, each contributing his special competence to the total task.*

The curriculum is in constant need of study and evaluation to make sure it is geared to current educational objectives and is making use of the best means available for attaining them. A review once every five years is not too often. Recommendation 17 calls attention particularly to subject matter, which is one basis for curriculum planning.

Traditionally, the disciplines provided the pattern for the school curriculum. But in the twentieth century, the study of human development, educational psychology, and educational sociology resulted in a new approach to curriculum planning. 51

The needs of society and of the learner were emphasized; the nature and structure of the disciplines were given less attention.

In recent years, the pendulum has begun to swing back. The disciplines, as major bases for structuring the school curriculum, are receiving thoughtful attention from scholars in various fields of knowledge and from educators at work in the schools. But a return to the disciplines is not regarded as a return to memorization of knowledge in any given subject area. Nor is it regarded as a construction project in which academic scholars, supported by a labor force of elementary and high school teachers, build concrete walls to protect abstract ideas in one field of knowledge from associating with congenial ideas in another field. On this latter point, however, some uneasiness persists. There are those, for example, who look on social studies in the elementary school as the illegitimate offspring of an unhallowed union between history and geography.

Concern for knowledge and for knowing, presumably imbedded in the subject-matter disciplines, is evident in many statements of educational objectives: "to develop an appreciation of the role of science in improving man's quality of living," "to develop an understanding of and appreciation for scientific method," "to develop skill in applying the methods of science to the practical problems of everyday living."

The public tends to be interested in the immediate utility of subject matter. This necessitates a practically determined part of the curriculum and influences the decisions educators and academic scholars make about the use of content and method from the disciplines. Schwab puts it this way in a working paper prepared for the Project:[13]

> . . . it is beyond all bounds of possibility that we can, in the schools alone, teach the disciplines and impart the semi-disciplines by which the lay public can extract unaided what it needs from the disciplines for present needs. Hence, there should be, not only mathematics as set theory, but mathematics as simple arithmetic calculation, as simple factoring of equations, as information about the more useful properties of curves and angles. There should not only be physics as a construction of elegant theories of atomic structure and as the derivation of theorems and equations from

fundamental conservation laws and basic constants but also physics as the behavior of levers and dynamos, vacuum tubes and atomic energy plants. In biology, there is not only the almost-elegance of genetics and evolution, but also some simple consequences of our misbehavior with respect to natural resources; some facts and simple ideas about medicines, digestive tracts, sewage disposal, fluorine and water supplies, diet and cleanliness.

Schwab goes on to point out, as have others before him, that the pursuit of science, of systematic knowledge of subject matter, is more practical than the "practical."[14]

> Its vast superiority lies in the fact that it enables us to *anticipate* practical problems, not merely to wait until they are upon us. It provides for our future as well as our present. For scientific knowledge is knowledge ready and available of the stuff, the things, the doings, the undergoings, of which we inevitably must forge all our know-hows.

For several decades, schools have tended toward a practicality in the curriculum. Learnings that appeared to have no immediate practical utility have been justified by dreaming up human activities in which the specific learnings might have a clearly visible use. A bit of subject matter such as square root is justified for its practical application to building a set of wooden steps; a whole subject matter such as trigonometry is justified for its application to the reading of maps. Learnings which would have ultimate applicability in many aspects of human behavior and welfare, *if seen as part of a whole syntactical structure,* are thus prostituted to the ends of immediate practicality. Obstacles are thrown in the way of learners ever coming to see the truly practical character of the discipline, the ultimate practicality that both exceeds and envelops immediate practicality.

Inclusion of the disciplined component of the curriculum can, in fact must be, justified on the argument that the layman is both the consumer of knowledge and the supporter of its inclusion in the curriculum. Schwab's argument for such justification runs as follows:[15]

> Because the layman is a consumer and not a producer of knowledge, he needs enough of each discipline to understand the *kind*

of knowledge it produces, the sense in which it is verified knowledge, and the location of its growth points—the places at which it is least complete, or most susceptible of revision.

. . . The layman needs to know where the growth points of a discipline are located (and why they are growth points) because ignorance of them will mean that what he learned about a discipline in his schooling will otherwise collapse around his ears.

. . . Because the layman is the ultimate user of knowledge, the man who must act and undergo, he needs a view of the discipline from another vantage point. For actors and undergoers are better as they know what they are doing and why. Blind obedience to a routine, unquestioning obeisance to authoritative instruction produces inflexible actors and supine undergoers, neither of which are adequate to the rate of change which our technology and our ways of living now demand. The layman as giver of assent and cash support must see the disciplines from still a third angle. He must understand something of the sweat, patience, ingenuity, and insights which go into their making. He must understand something of their immediately material value to his pleasure and comfort. Otherwise he will not give his assent and his cash. Enquiry will languish, hence the resources of technology will not be replenished; thus our ability to solve our continuing stream of problems will fail. Finally, the layman, as a possible member of a discipline, needs a view of the discipline from still a fourth point of view. He needs to see, first, the kinds of skills and opportunities for individual action which each affords and rewards. Second, at some point, he needs a glimpse of the unsolved problems to which he, as a possible member, might contribute.

Deciding between practical and disciplined components of the curriculum is one issue in considering the place of subject matter in the curriculum organization. There are many others. Which bodies of content should be taught? How should the content be organized for learning? When should various learnings be taught? How can knowledge about learners and the learning process be used effectively?

These are problems for academic scholars and for scholars in the profession of teaching. Subject matter specialists must come to grips with consideration of human development when they approach the tasks of curriculum planning. Similarly, the most child-centered curriculum worker must face the demonstrated usefulness of principles drawn from subject-matter disciplines.

These and other issues related to the problem of what to teach must be considered thoughtfully as curriculum areas are studied systematically by classroom teachers, school administrators, scholars in the profession of teaching, academic scholars, and informed laymen, each group recognizing its specific role and contributing its special competence. The mathematics scholar, for example, can give valuable assistance to the teacher in identifying pertinent up-to-date content and concepts to be taught, but he should exercise caution in suggesting how to teach his subject to eight-year-olds. The elementary school teacher, on the other hand, should not be expected to make new discoveries in mathematical theory. But he should work with the educational psychologist and the curriculum specialist in deciding what new mathematics the eight-year-old can and should learn, and how best to teach it to him.

RECOMMENDATION 18 *In making selections of content, school staffs should study the results and recommendations of curriculum projects sponsored by nationally oriented groups with a view to applying promising findings.*

National curriculum projects

There should be a systematic procedure for studying the results of these curriculum projects. The procedure should recognize the importance of balance and continuity in the total school experience of students and include the steps prerequisite to curriculum changes.

Illinois math . . . PSSC . . . SMSG . . . the FLES program . . . the Economic Task Force—these and a bewildering number of other new terms are finding their way into the educational vocabulary. They refer to major curriculum studies that merit thoughtful consideration. The studies have grown, in part, out of the need to bring the school curriculum up-to-date so that new knowledge can be incorporated and obsolete content can be 55 eliminated. Most of the projects have focused on the development of materials for the secondary school; few have given attention to the elementary school program. In many instances, a broad range of teaching materials has been developed. Curriculum outlines developed by the staff are supported by staff-developed experimental textbooks, teachers' manuals, and films.[16]

The ways in which these studies are conducted and the recommendations that come from them deserve careful study. Educators cannot afford to accept the recommendations from these studies uncritically. Neither can they afford to reject them off-hand without thoughtful consideration. Most of the nationally oriented curriculum projects have had the advantage of rich resources, and in many instances recommendations have been tried out on an experimental basis in selected schools. The extent and soundness of these experiments have varied from project to project, and this fact should be taken into account in assessing reports of the experiments. A systematic procedure to follow in considering use of these studies may be helpful. The following steps are suggested for the school staff:

1. Survey the school's existing program to determine what consultant services from academic and educational specialists are needed. Give special attention to continuity and comprehensiveness of the present program.

2. Study, with assistance of guidance personnel, the range of abilities, backgrounds, and post-high-school goals among the student body. Learn, for example, what proportion of the students are college-bound or are capable of college training. Consider special factors in the local situation that influence the future educational goals of students.

3. Study the new program or programs that are available, with the picture of the school's current situation clearly in mind. In addition to this review, consider characteristics of the student population for which the new program was designed and study the results of field tests that were used in developing the program. This provides one basis for deciding to whom, in each student body, the new course or program might be offered profitably. Consider balance in the total

curriculum and sequential continuity in the particular field of study.

Call upon academic and educational specialists to assist in analyzing the recommended program. Take time for a thorough study and a thoughtful adaptation. Unless the need is recognized for a new program and people are willing to try it, chances for success are limited.

4. Prepare the ground for the new program through workshops or study groups. Include consultant help from both academic and educational specialists.

5. Explain to parents and other interested citizens the proposed changes in the curriculum and the reasons for them. Communicate with parents through PTA meetings and newsletters. In some cases, parent seminars for those who wish to explore the new materials are useful.

6. Evaluate the new program at the end of the first semester, the first year, and at periodic intervals thereafter. Make adaptations and decisions about the continued use of the program on the basis of these reports. Inform parents of the results of this continuing evaluation.

Decisions about whether to use and how to use the results of national studies should be made at the local level by the educational staff. These decisions should be based on careful study of both the projects and the particular school system for whose students the decisions are being made. An intermediate step might be a regional or statewide study of the national projects conducted by state departments of education or by curriculum and instructional study centers in universities.

DECISION AREA IX   Organizing Content

How should the content of the curriculum be organized?

The process of organizing content requires decisions of three major kinds. First, there are decisions about arranging learnings in sequence so that one learning builds upon another. In making these decisions, one deals with the curriculum *vertically*. Second, there are problems of arranging learnings so that they support one another. In making these decisions, one views the curriculum *horizontally*.

School decisions about continuity and sequence (the vertical view) and about scope (the horizontal view) establish certain degrees of freedom and of restriction for the teacher. If, for example, the school decision is to combine English and social studies into a core curriculum, then teachers are not free to proceed as though such a decision had never been made. Teachers do, however, make specific decisions of scope and sequence in selecting classroom learnings for the core program.

The third major organizational decision is that of selecting topics or units of study, the organizing centers for learning. At the school level these decisions take various forms. Some are general; they require only that certain content be covered. Some are highly specific; detailed resource units specify outcomes, list books to be read, suggest sample examination questions, and sometimes indicate the degree to which teachers are encouraged or permitted to deviate from the prescribed units.

The extent of school planning and the nature of the specifications about the use of the plans determine the framework within which teachers carry on the instructional program. Such planning determines whether teachers develop their own resource units and make their own yearly, monthly, weekly, and daily schedules, or whether most of their decisions center on the specifics required for carrying out plans set up by the school.

The National Committee for the Project on Instruction makes this recommendation relating to the organization of curriculum content.

Bases for organizing content

RECOMMENDATION 19 *The content of the curriculum should be organized in such ways that students may progress, from early to later school years, toward an increasingly mature utilization and organization of their knowledge. Helping learners see interrelationships and achieve unity from the diversity of knowledge is basic to any organization of content.*

School staffs should experiment with a variety of ways of organizing content. The nature, meaning, and structure of the discipline and differences in the ways students learn should be taken into account in selecting a particular plan of organization and evaluating its effectiveness.

Content selected for study should be organized to emphasize both the continuity of the selected threads of knowledge, values, and skills and the interrelationships among the threads. The geometric accumulation of knowledge and the rapid changes in man's way of structuring his insights rule out the school's traditional role as a mere transmitter of facts. The instructional quest must be for ways of inquiry that make the learner increasingly self-sufficient, and for principles, concepts, and theories that explain and interpret. Part of the job of education is to give direction to the process of internal integration, that process by which a diverse collection of knowledge and skills and values is woven together into patterns that influence the ways individuals think, feel, and act.

The National Committee recommends that the curriculum be organized in such ways that it provides opportunities for students to: (a) develop a broad range of knowledge, values, and skills, and (b) see the interrelationships among them. There are many possible ways of organizing the curriculum with these purposes in mind. Many different principles underlie the various patterns of content organization. Many different structures such as specific subjects, broad fields, and core arrangements are used in our schools. Some place emphasis on the learner, some on subject matter, some on both. Most of the organizing principles and structures now in use have some validity for some types of content; probably all of them have validity for some learners. But much careful experimentation and research are needed to test the effectiveness of organizing principles now in use and to discover new ones that may be effective.

Recommendation 19 contains broad suggestions for the organization of curriculum content. The National Committee urges

59

school staffs to experiment with different organizational patterns in order to discover those which seem most effective for achieving the educational objectives of the school. At every level, no matter how mature the student and how pure the content of the discipline, there is continuing need to help the learner see the interrelationships among various fields of knowledge.

SUMMARY

What knowledge, what skills, what values should the schools teach? For what purposes? To whom? When? In what order?

These are the kinds of questions that underlie the broad question of what to teach. They are basic and relatively unchanging—the answers are not. The answers change as society changes and as new knowledge is discovered. They change to reflect the beliefs, the values, and sometimes the prejudices of those who answer the questions. But the questions must be asked, again and again, and the best answers must be sought.

In this chapter, the National Committee for the Project on Instruction has dealt with seven questions that relate to decisions about what to teach. Briefly stated, these questions are concerned with the following problems:

- developing the potentialities of all members of the school population
- establishing priorities for the school: deciding what should be included in and what should be excluded from the school program
- identifying the school's role in dealing with national problems related to youth, such as youth unemployment and juvenile delinquency
- teaching about controversial issues and about communism and other ideologies
- providing and maintaining a balanced program for each individual
- selecting content to be taught
- organizing content

Each problem has been discussed briefly and has been followed by one or more recommendations that relate to the issues and are explained in slightly greater detail.

The discussion of the decision areas and of the recommendations has drawn upon the content of three supporting volumes: *Deciding What to Teach, Planning and Organizing for Teaching,* and *Education in a Changing Society.*

For a more detailed discussion of the material in Chapter 3, the reader is referred to the supporting Project volume, Planning and Organizing for Teaching. *John I. Goodlad was the principal writer of that report.*

⟨∾⟩

Chapter 3

PLANNING
AND ORGANIZING
FOR TEACHING

Americans in general and American educators in particular are perennially interested in the organizational aspects of school-keeping. Interest is heightened today, partly because of the sheer magnitude of our mass educational enterprise. The great numbers of children and youth pouring into our schools simply force attention to ways of organizing and classifying them for instruction. The amount of attention focused on organization suggests that some people may have deluded themselves into thinking that the problems of what and how to teach can be "organized away."

The interest in school and curriculum organization is being challenged anew by societal changes that affect both the nature of the organizational problems and the possibilities for solving them. There are more young people to be taught; there is more to be learned. More and more of the children and youth are in urban areas and many of them are newcomers to the city. Scientific and technological advances are rapid, filled with possibilities that often fascinate and sometimes frustrate the educator who tries to see their application to instructional and organizational problems.

But in spite of the continuing interest in organization, the organizational patterns used in our schools today are relatively few in number, too few to provide the alternatives that human 63 variability demands. Coexisting alternatives are essential. Without them, there can be neither useful comparisons nor convenient paths of departure for venturesome deviation.

The organizational patterns now in use and those that are currently emerging deserve thoughtful appraisal. "New" should not be identified automatically with "better," but neither should "old" be confused with "good." Bold and imaginative goals of education cannot be attained by means that are timid in approach and limited in vision. Their attainment requires systematic, sustained, and critical effort, uninhibited by the nostalgic memory of yesterday and accompanied by objective appraisal. This appraisal, not the absence of experiments and innovations to appraise, protects the time and talents of students and teachers.

Attention to ways of organizing the curriculum, the schools, the classrooms, and the instructional resources is timely, necessary, and wholesome. Analysis of the problems and issues involved is, however, a prelude to, not a substitute for, analysis of teaching and learning. This chapter and the supporting volume on which it is based bring the reader up to, but not into, a consideration of teaching and learning processes. This is not a discussion of teaching. It is an analysis of some of the planning behind teaching.

This chapter discusses three sets of problems related to planning and organizing for teaching: organizing the curriculum; organizing the school and the classroom; and organizing personnel, space, and materials.

DECISION AREA X   Organizing the Curriculum

How should the curriculum of the school be organized to give appropriate direction to the instructional process?

Decisions about organizing the curriculum should be based upon the learner, the subject matter, and the educational objectives to be achieved. Decisions made at the institutional level, the school or school system, give direction to teachers. These decisions indicate the framework of operation and suggest the instructional tasks to which the teacher should give his time. If

64

little curriculum planning is done at the school level, teachers are left to make a whole array of decisions, using such resources as are available.

Sound planning at the school level is essential. Individual teachers should not be left entirely on their own to make decisions which, taken cumulatively, are expected to produce desired outcomes in learners. Such anarchy results in a harum-scarum curriculum in which learners are directed first one way and then another. A framework is needed, a framework that gives systematic direction to the education of students and encourages coordination of the creative efforts of teachers.

In a study[17] of selected practices in elementary and secondary schools, conducted as part of the work of the Project on Instruction, school principals were asked to rank, in the order of their use, ten kinds of resources for developing the school program. They reported that textbooks outrank all other resources as aids used in developing the instructional program. Next in order, and not far behind the textbooks, come curriculum materials prepared by state departments of education, school systems, or local faculties. Reports by prominent educators and laymen rank much lower on this list of resources.

In this chapter, the framework for the school program is identified as an institutional or school plan of instruction of the type which principals in the survey ranked high as a resource for instructional improvement. Several basic decisions must be made in developing such school plans. If any one of them is neglected, balance in teaching and learning is endangered. Textbooks cannot carry the burden of these decisions; good school curricular plans can. Three recommendations related to curriculum planning at the school level are discussed in this chapter.

RECOMMENDATION 20   *The aims of education should serve as a guide for making decisions about curriculum organization as well as about all other*

Educational objectives   *aspects of the instructional program.*

The public, through the local school board, is responsible for determining the broad aims of education. The professional staff is responsible for   65

*translating the broad aims into specific objectives
that indicate priorities and define clearly the behaviors intended for the learners. The local board of
education has responsibility for seeing that an
acceptable statement of objectives and priorities is
prepared and for endorsing such a statement.*

A recent publication of the American Association of School
Administrators, NEA, contains the following statement:[18]

> The school board in the local district is the agency designated
> by the state to represent the people of the local district and the
> state. The board is charged with responsibility to interpret the
> educational needs and desires of the people and to translate them
> into policies and programs.

The responsibility of the board of education for seeing that
there is a clear statement of objectives to provide a sense of
direction to local schools would seem to be an obvious one.
Surprisingly, however, many local boards of education do not
accept this particular responsibility, perhaps because objectives
are sometimes mistakenly regarded as platitudinous statements
unrelated to the practical business of schoolkeeping. As a matter
of fact, many existing statements of objectives *are* filled with
meaningless generalizations and give little help in determining
priorities for the instructional program. Such statements are not
acceptable statements of objectives and priorities and have undesirable effects on the school program. Without criteria for
inclusion and exclusion of content and learning opportunities,
principals and teachers are technically free to teach almost anything that does not come under those political, economic, and
religious categories declared "closed" by various pressure groups.
In such circumstances, teachers and principals are harassed by
sponsors of essay contests, do-gooders, and a variety of salesmen,
all seeking to influence what is taught in the schools.

Both the layman and the educator are concerned with the
process of identifying the objectives of education, but they have
different roles. It is the prerogative of the American people,
under the auspices of state and federal agencies for education,

to determine the societal aims for education. These aims should identify both ends and means at broad levels of generality. At the local level, lay authorities must take full responsibility for the use they make of these aims as a data source in establishing specific goals for their schools. If they fail to set priorities or to account for the needs and the peculiarities of the local community and student body, they and they alone must be held accountable to the people.

The determination of institutional objectives, however, is the responsibility of top-level professional leadership. Valid objectives cannot be developed apart from data about learners as well as about society and organized knowledge. Such information is a vital part of the professional equipment of a teaching staff. The staff, therefore, has the responsibility for refining societal aims into institutional objectives, with behavior and content stated specifically. Within the framework of school objectives are the decisions related to immediate purposes: choosing specific topics for study, selecting instructional materials, and setting a pace appropriate to individual abilities within the group.

The task of formulating useful educational objectives is a difficult one. It is not, however, a job to be undertaken as though nothing like it had ever been done before and no help was available. There are innumerable resources, human and material. Systematic procedures should be used to identify these resources and to make effective use of them.

The objectives that are identified and formulated should be endorsed by the board of education. When school boards endorse the precise educational objectives developed by professionals, and this they must do at some point or be judged delinquent, they then become responsible for these objectives and for disseminating information about them.

RECOMMENDATION 21 *In each curricular area, the vertical organization of subject matter should take account of: (a) the logical structure of the subject; (b) the difficulty of material as related to the student's intellectual maturity; (c) the relation of the field to other fields.*

Curricular sequence

67

Procedures and instruments for evaluating pupil progress must be specifically geared to the school's educational goals and to the curricular sequence in use in the school.

In the Disciplines Seminar,[19] assembled in 1961 as part of the Project on Instruction, seventeen specialists in the humanities, the physical and biological sciences, and the social sciences reviewed the nature of their disciplines and the implications for curriculum planning in elementary and secondary schools. Three ideas, common to all presentations, came through forcefully. First, much of what is being taught is woefully out of date. Second, the mere substitution of new content for old is not the answer to updating the curriculum. Third, basic to each discipline are methods of inquiry and structures by means of which the field is organized for discovery, accumulation, and communication of knowledge. To understand the field in any general or specialized way, it is necessary to learn these methods and structures.

These ideas are not new, but because of the unprecedented expansion of knowledge since 1950, they take on unique significance for all aspects of school planning. If present school content and ways of organizing that content are out of date, then traditional patterns of curriculum organization must be examined critically. Patterns that encourage longitudinal, sequential exploration of the fields of knowledge should be encouraged. If it is important for students to learn to apply and synthesize knowledge, to explore many references, and to predict the consequences of their own actions, then patterns of curriculum organization should support the development of these skills.

The effectiveness of various patterns should be tested in terms of their influence on student learning, student behavior. Currently, adequate measuring instruments are not available for evaluating the effectiveness of patterns of organization that emphasize the long-term development of subject-matter structure and human behavior. And educators should beware of attempting to evaluate such patterns by measures that were designed to evaluate the more traditional curriculum structures. They should, rather, encourage the development of new instruments appropriate for measuring the effectiveness of new organizational patterns.

Tests are developed to meet educational demands. If educators are content to go on evaluating their efforts on the basis of a narrow, inappropriate range of test items, test manufacturers will continue to work within that narrow range. But if educators insist on having instruments that will yield information, for example, about how well students are able to discover, apply, and synthesize knowledge, there will be a prompt response from test designers and rapid advance in evaluative processes.

RECOMMENDATION 22 *The fact that very young children* can *learn relatively difficult aspects of science, mathematics, and other subjects is at best an incomplete answer to the question of whether they* should *learn them at this particular stage of their development. Decisions about* when to teach what *should be based on both the learner's ability to understand and the relative importance of alternative ways of using the learner's time at any given point in his school experience.*

When to teach what

The current pressure to push subjects further down in the curriculum deserves thoughtful attention from parents and educators. The sources of pressure should be understood and the validity and relevance of the reasons given for downward placement should be examined. The major reasons given in support of pushing subject matter lower in the curriculum are these:

• Children's ability to learn difficult content at an early age has been underestimated. It is possible for young children to learn aspects of subjects once thought appropriate only for later study.

• There is much to be learned and new knowledge is being discovered every day. One way to cope with this rapidly increasing body of knowledge is to teach more sooner.

- The society in which today's children will be adults will require high-level skills from its citizens. Children who have an early start in such subjects as science and mathematics will probably be the ones who get ahead most rapidly.

Before World War II, the theory was generally accepted that children's minds developed from one stage to another and that certain concepts could not be learned until the mind had developed biologically to the necessary level of complexity. For example, the child was not ready to learn to read until age six, to learn ancient history until ages eleven or twelve, or to learn algebra until the age of fourteen.

Recent research, however, has changed this view. The evidence indicates that children are capable of learning simplified aspects of any subject at almost any age. What they can understand, at any stage in their development, depends heavily on how it is explained and on what their background has been. These findings suggest that less reliance should be placed on estimates of biological maturation and greater emphasis should be placed on active stimulation of learning.

It is important to have the best evidence that can be collected about the influence of age or maturity level of the student upon success in learning particular skills and knowledge. It is equally important to look at this evidence objectively. An unsupported prejudice in favor of traditional placement of subject matter should not be allowed to block the view. If seven-year-old children can learn aspects of physics and mathematics, the curriculum planner needs to know this and take it into account. But decisions about when to teach what must rest in part upon value judgments about the best use of the learner's time. There is no logical progression from "Seven-year-olds *can* learn aspects of physics" to "Therefore, seven-year-old children *should* learn aspects of physics."

The fact that children can learn a great variety of things at an early age increases the alternatives that are available and complicates the problem of making choices. But choices must be made; there is not enough time to teach everything that can be learned.

In making decisions about when to teach what, curriculum

planners and teachers need to consider carefully such questions as the following:

- What are the reasons for the present placement of subject matter? Are they valid?
- What are the criteria for determining whether or not it is best to introduce a seven-year-old to a study of physics or geometry? What other learnings may be sacrificed if the new material is introduced?
- Does the early introduction result in more efficient learning later? If study were delayed for two or four or six years, would the learner, because of greater maturity, progress just as rapidly toward mastery as would the student who had the early introduction to the subject? Is there a difference from one area of study to another? For example, in terms of effect on later learning, is it more important to introduce foreign languages early than it is to introduce algebra in the early school years? Is there evidence on this point?

In making decisions about placement of content, teachers and curriculum planners need to consider the great differences among individuals and the importance of flexibility in instructional programs. The extent of such consideration will be reflected in the decisions. For example, the conclusion that "We should not teach geometry to *any* seven-year-olds" is quite different from "We should not teach geometry to *all* seven-year-olds." Realistically, the question is not just *when* to teach *what;* the question is *when* to teach *what* to *whom.*

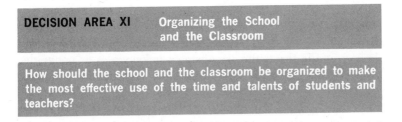

DECISION AREA XI   Organizing the School and the Classroom

How should the school and the classroom be organized to make the most effective use of the time and talents of students and teachers?

Is team teaching more effective than nongrading in providing for individual differences? Is ability grouping superior to grading   71 in fostering academic achievement? Is the self-contained classroom preferable to a departmentalized type of organization?

These and similar questions about school organization are often asked. They would be asked less often if there were better understanding about the purposes and functions of school organization and if there were general agreement on the meaning of terms used in discussing school organization.

Schools are organized to serve specific functions. They must classify students and move them upward from a point of admission to a point of departure. *Vertical* organization serves this function. Schools must also divide the student body among the available teachers. *Horizontal* organization serves this function. Confusion arises from failure to differentiate between vertical and horizontal aspects of school organization.[20]

Grading, multigrading, and nongrading are the vertical organization plans from which to choose. In the *graded school,* a rather specific body of subject matter and a rather specifically defined group of skills are assigned to each grade level. Students are expected to complete one year of work for one grade of vertical progress as they move through the school.

In the *multigraded school,* students who would ordinarily be classified in one of two or three sequential grades are assigned to a single class. A class of thirty children, for example, could include some children who would be in grade three under the graded system, some who would be in grade four, and some who would be in grade five. Because of variation in his ability and background, a child in this class may be working at three different grade levels—perhaps grade five for reading, grade three for arithmetic, grade four for social studies.

In the *nongraded school,* grade labels are removed from some or all classes. If grade labels are removed from kindergarten through grade three, the arrangement is known as a "nongraded primary unit." If grade labels are removed from the customary grades four, five, and six, the arrangement is called a "nongraded intermediate unit." The goal in nongrading is to provide opportunity for continuous progress for each learner. There is no set body of content or group of skills to be covered by each student within a prescribed period of time. Materials are selected to match the spread of individual differences in the instructional group, and students move upward according to their readiness to proceed.

For the *horizontal* organization of the school, there are many possible patterns. All of them, however, are derived from only three different kinds of considerations: the learner, the curriculum, the teacher.

If the primary consideration is the learner, then a choice must be made between homogeneity (likeness) and heterogeneity (difference) in the pupils who make up the class group. If the choice is for homogeneity among learners, the criterion of likeness may be age, size, interest, ability, achievement, or a combination of these and other factors.

If the primary consideration is the curriculum, a choice may be made between separate subjects and various combinations of subjects as the basis for setting up class groups.

If the primary consideration in establishing a pattern of horizontal organization is teacher qualification, one choice is between the self-contained classroom (one teacher for all subjects) and departmentalization (a different teacher for each subject).

Team teaching is one horizontal scheme that combines considerations of children, curriculum, and teacher qualifications in establishing class groups. The term "team teaching" is applied to so many different ventures in cooperative teaching that it has come to have many meanings. Communication might be improved if the term were used only to refer to cooperative teaching that has all three of the following characteristics: (1) a hierarchy of personnel—team leader, master teacher, clerk, and so forth; (2) a delineation of staff function based on differences in personal interests and preparation, or on the kinds of learning activities that have been planned; (3) flexibility in grouping the students who are under the supervision of the teaching team.

Schools often combine two or more kinds of horizontal organization. A high school, for instance, may be semidepartmentalized with a different teacher for each subject except for English and social studies which may be combined in a core curriculum and taught by one teacher.

It is important to keep in mind the fact that the over-all school 73 structure is a product of decisions on both vertical and horizontal organization. There may be literally dozens of possible patterns of over-all school organization. In a school that has a graded vertical structure, students may be grouped horizontally according to their presumed homogeneity in ability, achievement, interests, or study habits—or they may be grouped quite heterogeneously. Students may be grouped according to these same criteria in a school that has a nongraded vertical pattern. Some type of team teaching arrangement for horizontal interclass grouping may be used in either a nongraded or a graded school.

A more detailed discussion of horizontal and vertical patterns of school organization appears later in this chapter. Attention is directed at that point to the relationship between school organization and educational function. Ideally, organization has no functions of its own. It exists to accommodate, support, and expedite the educational functions of the school; the primary virtue to be sought is that it "fit" or accommodate school functions.

That is the ideal, but schools do not exist in Utopian surroundings. In the United States, they exist in a generally supportive but nonetheless questioning society that is concerned with efficiency and with dollars and cents. Proposals for new or modified forms of school organization must do more than promise compatibility between form and function; they must also stand tests of efficiency. Innovations are accepted slowly even when their educational virtues are many and obvious. They are accepted still more slowly, or rejected, if they are difficult to administer or expensive in terms of time and money.

Educators should be able to justify widespread adoption of such organizational devices as nongraded or multigraded schools, flexible student grouping, and team teaching on practical grounds of efficiency as well as on theoretical grounds of desirability. But they should also be given freedom and encouragement to experiment with changes in organizational patterns. Many promising possibilities for improving the instructional program will inevitably be lost if educational changes and innovations are ruled out prematurely because they do not immediately offer more in learning product or because they initially cost more than conventional practices.

The National Committee for the Project on Instruction makes five recommendations about school and classroom organization. None of these recommendations can be explained and discussed apart from consideration of significant facts about learners themselves. To provide the necessary background and avoid repetition, some relevant information about learners is presented here, ahead of the specific recommendations. These facts might appear to be obvious but they are too frequently ignored when educational decisions are made.

THE STUBBORN FACT OF INDIVIDUAL DIFFERENCES

Human variability is real, inevitable, ineradicable, desirable, and, indeed, essential. Some of this variability shows up in individual differences in ability and desire to learn and in ways of learning. The differences exist within individuals as well as among them, and they complicate the problem of school organization. They complicate it in part because the central problem in school organization is to promote the greatest possible *individual growth* and learning within a *group setting*.

No scheme of school or curriculum organization washes away human variability or the manifold problems of dealing with it instructionally. This being so, much organizational effort clearly is misplaced. Organization cannot eliminate individuality—that is impossible and undesirable. But it can illuminate individuality so that human ingenuity will be more likely to come to terms with it.

Differences Among Individuals

Children entering kindergarten or first grade differ from one another markedly in their readiness to profit from particular learning opportunities. Intelligence tests provide one measure of these differences. They reveal a spread of about four years in mental age within a group of six-year-olds entering the first grade. In other words, some of these six-year-olds compare with average four-year-olds in their intellectual equipment. Others are more like average eight-year-olds. The spread between the quick and the slow increases with time, just as a fast car steadily increases its lead on a slow one. When these youngsters enter the fifth grade, a few of them compare favorably in mental age with high school freshmen and a few have developed no further in their ability to use language and manipulate number symbols than have most children still in the first grade.

Learners vary widely in their school achievement. The spread in *average* achievement in an elementary school class slightly exceeds the number of the grade level. Thus the spread is more than three years in a third-grade class, four years in a fourth-grade class, and so on. By the junior high school years, this overall spread is estimated to be approximately two-thirds of the mean age of the grade group. The mean age for a group of children entering the seventh grade is approximately twelve years. The spread in achievement, then, is eight years—from the third grade to the eleventh. Using the same formula, the spread among all youth entering their junior year in high school would be from the elementary school to the graduate school!

Class groups spread out like this on any yardstick one chooses to use in measuring them. Some people conclude, therefore, that students should be grouped for instruction on the basis of some criterion of likeness or homogeneity. But these data are all about differences between and among individuals. The data on differences within an individual are equally sobering and shake one's confidence in any across-the-board mechanism of school organization.

Differences Within Individuals

The most compelling evidence about human variability is found within the individual—under the skin of one person. For decades it has been known that children vary within themselves in mental abilities as well as in other ways. One child reads well and calculates poorly; another calculates well and reads poorly. Yet if their test scores are averaged, the two appear to be equal in educational achievement.

Variation exists within the individual with respect to different competencies; variation also exists within the individual from age to age. Interests and attitudes may change and significantly influence test results.

The sharp differences in interests and abilities within one child should warn parents and teachers against making flat assumptions about the potential of a person who is identified as "average" or "superior" or "low" in intelligence. Youngsters of average intelligence often outclass their genius level peers in arriving at novel solutions to problems. Young people who break with tradition in the creative way they manipulate art media are sometimes indifferent scholars.

The correlation between intelligence and achievement test scores is far from perfect. The student at the top of the list in achievement often is a third of the way down in IQ; those with the highest IQs may rank at the midpoint of the class group in achievement.

Differences in achievement from subject field to subject field within a single learner are even more striking. Few children are at grade level in all subjects when measured on achievement tests. Midyear achievement test scores reveal that only three or four children in an elementary school class of thirty are at grade level in all subjects. The remaining 80 to 90 per cent of the children range from several grades below to several grades above their grade placement. A teacher who says, "I teach the fourth grade," is usually talking about only three or four children in the class!

Students with high or low averages often deviate markedly from these averages in one or more fields. A slow-learning child in the fourth grade, with average achievement of second grade, ninth month, may score fourth grade, first month in arithmetic computation but only first grade, fourth month in paragraph meaning. Another child in the fourth grade, with average achievement of fifth grade, second month, may score third grade, ninth month in arithmetic computation, and seventh grade, fourth month in paragraph meaning.

In what grades do these two "fourth-grade" children belong? If grade placement is to be based on achievement, each child belongs in several grades. The first child belongs in the second grade for reading and the fourth for arithmetic; the second child belongs in the third for arithmetic and the seventh for reading. But where does one set the limits? For arithmetic, the first child   77 is about to move into the third grade and the second child into the fourth. Should they be transferred if it is only midyear?

If all learners are moved subject-by-subject, there will be great ranges in chronological age, social maturity, and interests. Should ten-year-olds who read at the second-grade level be placed with six-year-olds who read at the second-grade level? What about the fourth-grader reading at the seventh-grade level? Is he to be transported to the junior high school? When such questions as these are considered, subject-by-subject classification as the answer to the question of appropriate grade placement slips into obscurity—except for would-be school reformers who have not thought the problems through in the light of appropriate data.

The foregoing data about learners have to be taken into account in making intelligent decisions about school and classroom organization. They are reflected, directly or indirectly, in the recommendations that follow.

VERTICAL ORGANIZATION

The National Committee for the Project on Instruction makes the following recommendation about the vertical organization of the school.

Nongrading, multigrading, grading

RECOMMENDATION 23   *The vertical organization of the school should provide for the continuous, unbroken, upward progression of all learners, with due recognition of the wide variability among learners in every aspect of their development. The school organization should, therefore, provide for differentiated rates and means of progression toward achievement of educational goals.*

Nongrading and multigrading are promising alternatives to the traditional graded school and should be given careful consideration in seeking to provide flexible progress plans geared to human variability.

Differing assumptions about school function, about what should be taught, and about individual differences lead to different patterns of vertical school organization. Some lead to grading, some to multigrading, some to nongrading.

The assumptions made by the National Committee are these:

• The instructional program of the school should be designed to develop the potentialities of all members of the school population, as individuals and as members of society.

• The instructional program should include the learning of basic generalizations and the development of ways of knowing and thinking.

• The vertical pattern of school organization should provide for the continuous, unbroken, upward progression of all learners, with due regard for the great range of differences among and within them.

Three patterns of vertical organization are examined here to see if they serve these educational functions.

The Graded School

Grading has been the traditional way of organizing schools for the vertical progression of students. The graded school was introduced in this country a little over a century ago, roughly, 1848. At that time, people believed that the needs of society and of the learner could be served by a relatively simple program of elementary education. Knowledge and skills available to the learner, and needed by him, were much more limited than they are today. It seemed a reasonable undertaking to select and package certain fundamental skills and knowledge to make up an elementary education. Furthermore, insights into basic differences in learning were limited. It was assumed that differences in accomplishment were primarily the result of differences in willingness to apply oneself. The motto was, "If at first you don't succeed, try, try again."

Underlying the graded school there are three main assumptions: (a) elementary and secondary schools should "cover" a specific body of subject matter; (b) this subject matter should be identified and rigorously prescribed; and (c) individual differ- 79 ences merely determine one's chances of success in the race to cover the prescribed material. The pattern of vertical school structure is laid out in grades and a rather specific body of subject matter is assigned to each grade level. Textbooks are prepared for the grade; teachers are categorized as "first-grade," "second-grade," "fifth-grade." The common denominator is a year of work for a grade of vertical progress. Nonpromotion is a primary mechanism by which students who progress slowly are adjusted to the system.

Once established, the graded form of vertical organization created several auxiliary functions: the functions of determining content for graded texts, questions for graded achievement tests, and grade-level expectations for students, teachers, and parents. These grade-level expectations have become part of our culture. More than graded structure itself, they have been responsible for preserving graded curricular and instructional practices. To attempt to change graded structure without changing graded expectations is to insure the continuation of the graded school no matter what new name may be attached to the effort to get away from it.

In spite of its firm hold on our educational system, the graded system has been under criticism almost from the beginning. The mold had scarcely stiffened before some educators began to question it, contending that the graded "lock-step" denied individuality, stifled initiative, and unjustly punished the willing but slow. Many experimental plans to modify grade-by-grade progression were conceived, but most of them grew and died without reproducing their kind. The graded system, efficient for classifying large numbers of students, became standard practice.

The most serious threat to the graded plan, however, came not from without but from within. It soon became apparent that all six-year-olds are not equally capable, and that accomplishment is not merely a matter of effort. Many children simply did not learn what was expected of them in the first grade, or the fourth, or the sixth. The answer was to require them to do the work over, to repeat the grade. Those who were slow to learn were not promoted. "If at first you don't succeed, do it over."

The answer was more obvious than accurate. As early as 1909,

Ayres[21] pointed to the additional school costs incurred by high nonpromotion rates and implied that the practice should not continue if it could not justify itself through improvements in educational accomplishment. Recent research shows that nonpromotion does not result in improved educational accomplishment. Nonpromoted children achieve no more than their promoted counterparts. In fact, there is a greater tendency for nonpromoted children to do less well a year after nonpromotion than they did on comparable tests a year earlier.

There are still other reasons for being critical of the graded system and nonpromotion practices when the further dimension of social and personal well-being is added. Research evidence indicates clearly that nonpromotion does not enhance pupil adjustment. Studies of matched groups show that promoted pupils are more acceptable to their peers, less often reported for disciplinary offenses, and more likely to wish to continue with their schooling.

Research evidence indicates that the graded structure does not give effective support to the concept of education it was designed to serve. But, apart from that, it is only reasonable to conclude that a pattern of organization intended to support one set of assumptions about education and the learner will not fit assumptions that are sharply different. The assumptions underlying the graded structure are fundamentally at odds with the assumptions, listed on page 79, made by the National Committee about school function and the learner.

Multigrading

Periodically, attempts are made to modify or depart from graded structure. One such modification is multigrading. In multigrading, assumptions about school function and about what should be taught are comparable to the assumptions underlying the graded structure, but the assumptions about the implications of individual differences are not the same. Differences in ability and accomplishment among learners are recognized, and the pattern of school organization seeks to differentiate progress according to these differences.

The lock-step of graded structure is modified into a multigrade plan. But subject-matter demarcations, sometimes called "levels," are retained and often are used as a basis for horizontal groupings. Departmentalization of instruction according to subjects is common, particularly in and above the upper elementary years. In fact, this pattern of organization tends to produce a fairly inflexible grouping by subjects. Nonpromotion disappears, but progress is stepped up for students who complete their schooling in fewer years and slowed down for those who need more time to complete elementary and secondary education.

In multigrading, students classified in one of two or three sequential grades are assigned to a single class. Take a group of ninety children, for example, thirty of whom would ordinarily be assigned to grade three, thirty to grade four, and thirty to grade five. Instead of following this method of grouping, the children may be distributed so that ten from each grade are in each of three classes. Within each class, a child may be in three grades—grade five for reading, grade three for arithmetic, grade four for social studies.

This system of multigrade grouping is one way to provide for individual differences. It creates a school structure that requires teachers to provide for more than one grade level at any given time. Individual differences over and above those represented in the three-grade range are handled within the class.

Multigrading, like grading, requires all learners to cover essentially the same body of material, but it permits students to move at different rates of speed. The key difference between grading and multigrading is that multigrading makes some school-wide organizational provision for differentiating the progress of learners. The reorganization that occurs in moving from grading to multigrading is geared to gross differences among all learners. It usually provides for the rather extreme deviation among individuals at both ends of a continuum; the large group of students between the two extremes is affected in only minor ways.

Multigrading brings with it several interesting concomitants:

- A teacher *may* transfer the entire group of three grades to another teacher, but it is convenient sometimes to transfer only a portion of the group and to receive a like number of children from other classes.

- The presence of three grades in a single class and the movement of children from one grade to another within the class tend to emphasize individual differences and force provision of learning opportunities more in line with these differences. This makes parents aware of the fact that a single child advances at different rates of speed in different aspects of his learning.
- Retention of the grade label avoids a sharp break with the past and continues the use of terminology familiar to everyone.

Nongrading

As indicated earlier, nongrading is an arrangement in which grade labels are removed from some or all classes. An entire school may be nongraded, or, within a school, there may be a nongraded primary unit or a nongraded intermediate unit.

Theoretically, grading and nongrading are the polar opposites among alternatives for vertical school organization. In *pure* grading, the content of the instructional program and its sequential arrangement are determined by assigning subject matter to various grade levels, designating instructional materials for particular grade levels, and promoting pupils upon satisfactory completion of the work specified for each grade level. In *pure* nongrading, the sequence of content is determined by the difficulty of the subject matter and the student's ability to cope with it. Instructional materials are varied to match the spread of individual differences within the instructional group, and students move upward according to their readiness to proceed. Promotion or nonpromotion does not exist as such; continuous progress for each learner is the important goal.

The nongraded school is characterized by central concern for *the* individual and *all* individuals. As viewed from this learner-centered perspective, the first function of the school is to develop the unique potentialities of all students. This focus on the learner does not deny the place of subject matter. Knowledge and skills are needed and used for developing the maximum potential of the learner, but a body of subject matter to be "covered" is not rigidly prescribed.

83

The philosophy of the nongraded school is held by many teachers who work in graded schools and is reflected in their approach to instruction. In their concern for the individual and individuality, it is usually necessary for these teachers to reject the traditional denotations of grades. The idea that the curriculum should consist of subject matter laid out in grade-level patterns to be covered by all cannot live with a continuous-progress-of-each-learner approach to curriculum and teaching. If teachers believe in a learner-centered approach and act in harmony with their belief, it is necessary for them to modify some of the standard practices associated with grade structure. They use grade designations only as group labels for convenience in keeping records, locating pupils, transferring data and pupils to other schools, and so on. Literally, they destroy the meaning of "grade," and a nongraded school emerges although it is still called "graded."

The teacher who teaches in a graded school but is philosophically committed to nongrading is caught up in a number of vexing dilemmas. Grade-level expectations are built into curricular patterns and structural organization. They are built into the thought processes of children, parents, and colleagues, and into the materials and tests used each day. To ignore these expectations is to invite misunderstanding and often condemnation. The teacher, for example, who asks for several different sets of books instead of a single series of texts is likely to encounter the query of a well-meaning but noncomprehending colleague: "Why must special provisions be made for you? Why can't you be like the rest of us?" Not every teacher, however conscientious, has the physical and emotional stamina to fight the battle for personal acceptance and to engage in the sheer hard work required to be different. It is often less wearing to go along with the prevailing pattern.

A reverse situation occurs when teachers in a school that has become nongraded are not sympathetic with or sufficiently knowledgeable about the educational philosophy of nongrading. The removal of grade labels is no guarantee that teachers will take advantage of the opportunities nongrading is intended to provide. To change from graded to nongraded, a school has to make appropriate changes in point of view, program, and structure. A school with only grade labels removed is nongraded in name only. Literally, it is still a graded school.

Exponents of nongrading claim benefits with respect to pupil well-being and achievement which have not been proven conclusively. Critics of the nongraded plan claim that what nongrading purports to do can be accomplished as readily in graded schools. To date, the research is inadequate and inconclusive. Some studies favor graded schools, some favor nongraded schools, and some show no significant differences between the two.

The crucial inadequacy of most such studies is the failure to identify two sets of characteristics by which nongraded and graded schools may be clearly differentiated. Consequently, the researchers often are not making a valid comparison. In several studies, for instance, ability or achievement grouping was being used in the sample of nongraded schools but not in the graded schools used for comparison. Are differences among pupils in these schools the product of graded or nongraded practices, or are they the product of ability grouping?

Nongrading is a vertical plan of school organization. It cannot be compared with ability grouping or any other scheme of horizontal organization. Failure to understand this difference leads to meaningless comparisons of organizational plans and to misleading conclusions about them.

Form and Function in Vertical Organization

Changes in school structure are meaningless if they are divorced from a conception of what the school is for. School leaders who consider modification of vertical school organization without an accompanying re-examination of school function should proceed with care. A new form of organization will not in itself change school function or substance. But thoughtful consideration of existing organizational patterns raises the question of compatibility among the various parts of schooling and creates opportunities for rethinking the whole of education.

In the absolute sense, there is no *best* pattern of vertical school organization. In the relative sense, the best pattern is the one   85 that most efficiently serves the functions of the school. If mastery of specific subject matter predominates as the goal, and if individual differences are regarded simply as defining the chances for student success, then graded content, graded materials, and graded expectations follow. The danger under such a system is in assuming that nonpromotion is an effective adjustment mechanism. It is not.

If emphasis on mastery of subject matter is coupled with desire to encourage differentiated rates of progress through a common set of learnings, then some modification of graded structure is called for. A multigrade plan or a nongraded plan warrants attention.

For all their good intentions, educators fall far short of their best dreams. A concept of education that sees the ends and means of schooling as growing out of primary concern for and insight into the nature of man and the welfare of the individual is still on the experimental frontier. It has yet to be implemented outside of experimental situations. The graded school, as traditionally defined and developed, does not appear to be the form best suited to maximum development of the individual. If grade norms are to serve as the device for classifying student progression through the school, their meaning must be revised radically and this is not easy to do. Similarly, existing nongraded patterns must be altered since the schools in which they exist tend to be modifications of graded schools rather than truly nongraded structures. Obviously, there is much yet to be done in devising new structural forms to fit the functions appropriate to tomorrow's schools.

HORIZONTAL ORGANIZATION

Problems of organizing schools horizontally should be differentiated sharply from problems of organizing schools vertically. Vertical organization provides a system for classifying students and moving them upward from entry into school until departure from it. Horizontal structure provides a system for dividing a given student population into instructional groups and allocating these students to teachers.

A major question in horizontal organization is: Should students be assigned in groups to a single teacher responsible for all of their instruction or should they be rotated among several teachers? For decades, the issue has been treated as much more settled for secondary schools than for elementary schools. Essentially, this is the issue of *departmentalized* versus *self-contained* classrooms.

Another continuing question is: Should students be grouped randomly or on some criterion of homogeneity such as ability, present attainments, interest, or learning style?

The elementary-school pattern of horizontal organization has been subject to cycles of criticism and variation. In theory, the self-contained classroom provides a teacher per group for the entire range of instructional activities. In practice, however, instruction in so-called self-contained classrooms frequently is taken over by various special resource persons. This is particularly true in large cities and suburban communities.

The opposite of complete self-containment is complete departmentalization. Students or teachers or both shift according to a precise time schedule so that each subject is taught by a different person, hopefully, a specialist. Most commonly today, primary grade classes (kindergarten through three) are self-contained most of the day. Special instruction, usually in art, music, and physical education, is provided according to the availability of personnel. The upper grades tend more often to be departmentalized, although the homeroom teacher usually teaches all subjects with the exception of art, music, and physical education. When the elementary school includes grades seven and eight, existing patterns in these grades are described more accurately as departmentalized rather than as self-contained. Students usually are taught by three or more teachers during the day.

The problem of horizontal organization at the elementary-school level is even more complicated by the issue of homogeneous versus heterogeneous grouping. Classes can be (and often are) self-contained but are made up of pupils who are grouped together according to criteria of ability or achievement. Classes can be (and sometimes are) departmentalized and students segregated first by subjects and then by some criterion of homogeneity in achievement or ability. For obvious reasons, schools that practice departmentalization and ability grouping simultaneously tend to be large. In fact, it is difficult to practice ability grouping in graded schools unless there are at least two classes at each grade level.

Horizontal organization of the school needs to satisfy criteria pertaining to subject matter and curriculum planning. For some years ahead, specialists in the several disciplines will be seeking to sell their wares to elementary and secondary schools. This is all to the good and overdue. But there is danger that schools will be submerged in the disciplines. The promising answer to the present curricular ills in precollegiate education is not a collection of twenty or more subjects from the kindergarten through high school. The answer is more likely to resemble a core of common learnings for the elementary school, perhaps not too sharply differentiated by subject-fields, and increasing opportunity for electing branches of this core for specialization toward the upper years of the high school.

It follows, then, that horizontal patterns of school organization must encourage a certain unity among learnings. If, for example, junior high school students are to pursue four or five major divisions of knowledge taught by a like number of teachers, the pattern of grouping these students for instruction must encourage communication among these teachers and, hopefully, meaningful correlation among the several fields. In determining these groupings, criteria pertaining to student achievement may take a secondary position to criteria of curricular scope and student style or pattern of learning.

The National Committee for the Project on Instruction makes four recommendations about horizontal organization.

RECOMMENDATION 24   *The assignment of pupils to classroom groups should be based on knowledge about students and teachers and on understanding of goals to be achieved.*

Bases for ability grouping

Efforts to set up groups in terms of ability and/or achievement do little to reduce the over-all range of pupil variability with which teachers must deal.

However, selective grouping and regrouping by achievement sometimes is useful, particularly at the secondary-school level.

In any school, there are students, teachers, and space. The setting up of class groups (interclass grouping) is a practical necessity, if only to utilize effectively both the available teachers and the available space.

Homogeneous grouping is a practice wherein the total student population is divided into instructional groups according to some criterion of likeness. This criterion of likeness can be almost anything: height, weight, sex, IQ, achievement, interests, study habits, socioeconomic class, and on and on. There is some degree of heterogeneity in any group. This is assured by the facts of individual differences. But deliberate heterogeneous grouping attempts to bring students together according to dissimilarity rather than similarity.

Very few thoroughgoing attempts at heterogeneous grouping exist. Most of the class groups in our schools are quite homogeneous in regard to chronological age and socioeconomic status, although they are heterogeneous in regard to ability and achievement.

There is a recurring controversy between the advocates of homogeneous grouping based on achievement or ability and the advocates of more heterogeneous arrangements. The research-minded individual, faced with this controversy, asks himself, "What happens when students are grouped into this or that pattern according to some criterion of homogeneity?"

There are at least three different ways of answering the question. One way is to provide data about the groups after they have been put together on some criterion of homogeneity. A second kind of answer looks at outcomes: "What happens to the learners in this or that homogeneous pattern?" A third raises questions about values: "What outcomes are desired for the school? What kinds of intergroup relationships should prevail in a democracy?" Questions like these bring us back to the matter of school function.

The criterion most commonly used in seeking to establish homogeneous *ability* groups is IQ. As pointed out earlier, groups that are relatively homogeneous on IQ are not homogeneous on achievement. Goodlad and Anderson[22] cite the case of a fifth-grade class in which the IQ spread of 60 or more points normally found in heterogeneous classes had been cut in half by removing all pupils of IQ over 120 or under 90. The spread in achievement in this group differed very little from the spread usually found in a class where no such modification is made.

Most teachers are aware of the gross discrepancies between IQ distributions and achievement distributions in the classes they teach. Many pupils who rank toward the top in achievement are in the middle range on IQ distributions; many students with genius IQ are mediocre in their school accomplishments. In his review of the literature on ability grouping, Otto[23] concludes that the separation of students into two groups according to ability reduces the variability in achievement by only about 7 per cent. The variability is still about 93 per cent of what it was before. When three groups are formed, the range in achievement becomes approximately 83 per cent of what it was before such selection is made—a reduction of 17 per cent. The evidence seems to indicate that *ability* grouping does not reduce to an appreciable degree the variability in student achievement.

Another criterion used in seeking to establish homogeneous groups is *achievement*. There are two major bases for achievement grouping. The first is an average achievement score computed by compiling the results from all sections of an achievement test. This score combines all subscores in arithmetic reasoning, arithmetic computation, paragraph meaning, word recognition, spelling, and so on. The data on individual differences presented earlier in this chapter reveal that students are not consistent in their scores. A student in the seventh grade may be at the seventh-grade level in *average* achievement, but at the eleventh grade in an aspect of reading such as paragraph meaning and at the fifth in an aspect of arithmetic such as computation. These differences within individuals cannot be organized away through interclass grouping.

90   A much more precise basis for achievement grouping is one

wherein students are grouped according to their achievement in specific subjects. This is fairly common practice at the secondary school level where there often are several sections of mathematics, English, social studies, and other subjects. These sections sometimes are set up to provide a narrower range of pupil accomplishment in the group than would result from random assignment of students to classes. If there are ninety students enrolled for Algebra I, the range of average achievement in this subject in the usual heterogeneous class is reduced 66⅔ per cent by dividing the ninety into three homogeneous classes, *using the criterion of achievement in algebra.* A given student might move during the day from Section I in English to Section III in mathematics and then to Section II in social studies. In this arrangement, the pattern of horizontal organization is homogeneous according to pupil achievement and departmentalized according to curriculum design.

This subject-by-subject grouping ignores the facts of intra-subject differences in the same individual. That is, his algebra achievement test score is an average of several component skills in which he may have a range of achievement. Furthermore, critics of interclass grouping on the basis of achievement in each subject cite three practical objections, applying especially to elementary education. First, they object to the amount of class-to-class movement that is required as children go from one class to another. Regrouping for each subject may interfere with the development of strong morale and mutual influence within each group. Second, they maintain that the accomplishments of children in the early age brackets change quickly. A group that is relatively homogeneous at the beginning of instruction rapidly becomes more and more heterogeneous. Third, they point out that children of very different chronological ages are brought together because of similarity in accomplishment in a given subject. A ten-year-old is very different from a six-year-old, even if both children read at the second-grade level. Consequently, problems of dealing with individual differences are compounded rather than simplified.

What is the character of groups after students have been brought together on some criterion of homogeneity? Ability grouping based on IQ reduces achievement variability in a group only slightly. Likewise, achievement grouping based on *average* achievement falls far short of providing group homogeneity on anything since students vary so in their attainments. Grouping in specific subjects on the basis of student homogeneity in achievement does reduce group variability. This homogeneity can be refined more and more, to the extent that there are many students from whom to select in grouping and to the degree that very precise areas of learning are selected. Two hundred students of the same age can be grouped rather precisely when the criterion used is arithmetic computation. Of course, the groups will remain heterogeneous in regard to other attainments.

Team teaching

RECOMMENDATION 25 *In order to provide individually planned programs for learners, taking into account the specific objectives to be achieved, the horizontal organization of the school should permit flexibility in assigning pupils to instructional groups that may range in size from one pupil to as many as a hundred or more. Well-planned cooperative efforts among teachers—efforts such as team teaching, for example—should be encouraged and tested.*

All students do not learn in the same way. Furthermore, the same individual learns differently at different times and with different teachers. Some students profit most from lectures, at least at times; others profit from small group discussions. Some work best in groups of two's and three's; others profit most from an almost completely individualized approach. In the elementary school, students should have an opportunity to explore all of these approaches. In this way, they may build up a repertoire of learning skills that will be useful for dealing with the variety of teaching styles they will encounter later. As students proceed to the upper levels of schooling, they should be encouraged to select their own individual approaches to learning.

If flexibility in grouping for instruction is to be provided, school organization and instructional space must support it. For years, educators assumed that a classroom group of approximately thirty was a necessary starting point. The egg-crate design of school rooms and school buildings supported such an assumption. Educators assumed further that such a class would operate much of the time as a group of thirty, with subdivisions taking place largely to accommodate differences in achievement.

Today, however, educators' thinking and school buildings, also, are breaking out of this standardized concept. Exciting new possibilities are emerging. Administrators are forcing some changes through over-all school organization and through the construction of buildings that provide flexible space. Trump and Baynham have said: [24]

> The school of the future will recognize the relationships among various aspects of learning: what happens to students when they take part in small classes of 15 or less for purposes of discussion; when they work in a relatively independent manner in laboratories, libraries, and cubicles; or when they listen to or view a demonstration or explanation in the setting of large-group instruction.

Efforts are being made, too, to provide greater opportunity for teachers to work together. At all levels of education, from the elementary school through the university, teachers have tended to work alone, separated geographically and intellectually from one another. Building design, school organization, teacher education, and sometimes individual preference have all supported isolation of the teacher at the actual working level of instruction. This isolation blocks the effective interchange of knowledge about students—their abilities, their achievements, their specific needs, their unique ways of learning. It also obscures the special talents of individual teachers and limits the possibilities for wide use of these talents.

Today there are hopeful signs of cooperative efforts to remove these barriers to good instruction. Various forms of team teaching are being used to explore the possibilities of cooperation in working with groups of students. Such efforts, carefully planned, 93 should be encouraged and should be evaluated rigorously to determine their effectiveness for improving the quality of teaching and learning in both the elementary and the secondary school.[25]

Tomorrow's school will multiply the setting and the number of specially competent teachers that function in the teaching-learning process. Discussions among teachers and counselors in the setting of the teaching team will provide coordination of learning experiences provided for students.

Self-contained classroom

RECOMMENDATION 26 *The school should be organized in such a way that it provides opportunity for each student to: (a) experience continuity and relatedness in his learning, and (b) have a close counseling relationship with competent teachers who know him well. Various forms of organization should be explored to determine their effectiveness for these purposes.*

The contributions of specialized personnel should be used as students progress through the elementary and secondary school. At whatever point specialized personnel are brought into the instructional program, their work should be coordinated with and related to the total program.

The self-contained classroom in the elementary school has long been supported on the grounds that it provides: (a) opportunity for continuity and relatedness in learning; and (b) opportunity for a close teacher-pupil relationship to undergird the teaching-learning process. The National Committee recognizes the bases for these claims but feels that these educational advantages are not the exclusive possession of a particular form of organization.

The teacher's problem, at all levels of instruction, is to identify and make available the resources that will contribute most to the learning experiences of children. Some of these resources may be found in the teacher next door; some are available through specialized personnel who are not regular classroom teachers. Cooperative planning is needed to make the best use of such resources and to relate them to a total program. Such planning may take

94

place within the framework of a school that has self-contained classrooms; it may take place in team-teaching arrangements; it may take place in the departmentalized organization that prevails in most secondary schools.

Each of these forms of organization can support some measure of cooperative planning and provide for some interrelatedness of learning. But no type of organization, in and of itself, insures continuity and relatedness of learning. In the self-contained classroom, for example, the teacher is largely free from school-wide divisions of the instructional day. But in spite of this, the *curriculum* of the elementary school, like the curriculum of the high school, is basically departmentalized. Teachers teach reading, spelling, arithmetic, social studies, science, art, music, and physical education as separate subjects in separate blocks of time. The bells that punctuate the day in most high schools are silent, but many pupils still move from activity to activity according to a schedule and the clock.

The need of each pupil for a close counseling relationship with a number of teachers who know him well over a period of years is sharply related to success in achievement and to satisfaction in school experience. The one-teacher-per-class arrangement, characteristic of the self-contained classroom, facilitates a close relationship between teacher and student over a period of many hours throughout the school year. But the claim of the self-contained classroom to superiority on the score of a close teacher-pupil relationship is being challenged by some participants in team-teaching experiments. These teachers say they get to know the students better than they do in the self-contained classroom. The reasons for this, they say, are that they have more time to observe students at work without being personally involved and that they have opportunity to share and compare their observations with colleagues who work with the same students.

It is not intended here to damn or defend a particular type of organization. The important need is to strengthen the relationship between the ends of education and the means by which schools seek to achieve them. The National Committee believes that for continuity and relatedness in learning, close teacher-pupil relationships are important for each student. Educators, therefore, 95 need to be flexible and creative in discovering and using means by which these ends may be achieved.

<table>
<tr><td>Classroom grouping</td><td>RECOMMENDATION 27 *In schools where the classroom is the unit of organization, teachers should organize learners frequently into smaller groups of varying types and sizes. Decisions as to size and membership of such groups should be based on knowledge about learners and on the specific educational purposes to be served at a given time for each learner.*</td></tr>
</table>

Subdividing students in a classroom into smaller groups has no virtues in and of itself. It makes sense only when a particular grouping arrangement facilitates the attainment of a specific educational goal. Effective use of grouping requires the teacher to be clear as to purpose. With the purpose clearly in mind, the teacher has two major sets of variables to work with in determining the pattern of classroom grouping. These are the individuals themselves and the subject matter to be taught.

The basis for subdividing a class group has almost always been pupil achievement. Using standardized or self-made group tests or observations of daily pupil performance, teachers divide a class into two or more instructional groups. This practice has both strengths and weaknesses and should be accompanied by other techniques designed to eliminate or reduce the disadvantages.

One of the strengths is the insight teachers can develop into the persistence of individual differences. It is important for a teacher to discover through experience that no matter how many subgroups there are in a class—two, four, six, ten—there are still gross differences among the individuals in any one group.

One direction for improvement in the use of intraclass grouping is the deliberate creation of groups which are not based on achievement and which alternate with achievement groups within the same subject. For example, children in three different achievement groups in reading frequently have the same reading problem, even though they read at different levels. A productive technique, then, is to pull these children together in a group for special instruction on their particular problem—for example, phonetic analysis or some particular comprehension skill. After a period of intensive instruction, the teacher dissolves this group and sets up a new group based on some other reading problem. This becomes a kind of diagnostic, rather than achievement, grouping.

If the range of educational objectives is to be given proper attention, there should be many approaches to grouping within the classroom. If the purpose is simply to put before the group a common body of information to be used in various ways later, there is no need to subdivide the class for the teacher's lecture or for a film or television presentation. If the refinement of certain skills is called for, then, perhaps some over-all group plan must provide opportunity within it for each student to practice the behavior at his present level of competence. If the purpose is to develop skills of social interaction, then the size and duration of these groups should provide optimum opportunity for give and take.

Whatever the size of the group, the individual learner is the focal point. The reason for placing him in a particular subgroup of a particular size is to help him with some aspect of his learning. In this matter of classroom grouping, the future will probably witness less attention to achievement as the within-class pattern of grouping, less and less conformity in the design of class groups, and more provision for individual learners to proceed at their own tasks at their own rates of speed.

DECISION AREA XII	Instructional Materials, Technology, Space

How can the quality of instructional materials be improved? How can the products of modern technology be used effectively? How can space be designed and used to support the instructional program?

Improvements in equipment and techniques of communication, in design and construction, and developments in electronics are 97 moving from the theory and drawing-board stages into practical application in daily life. New concepts of space, time, and instructional resources emphasize new functional definitions of the roles of teachers and students. Students are given greater responsibility for self-instruction. Teachers are urged to emphasize their intellectual and professional functions and to make expanded use of technological tools and new media. School plants and schedules are being reorganized around space and time concepts which emphasize the goals of students and teachers.

All of the newer concepts of space, time, and instructional resources facilities should be developed in a context of freedom and variety in solutions, emphasis on instruction, development of the individual's functional capacities, and application of technological solutions and multimedia approaches to learning. Changes in the curriculum should take into account the extent to which the available resources of educational materials, the physical settings, and the technology can limit or advance the goals of education.

The National Committee for the Project on Instruction has delved into these questions because it feels that no school can or should ignore their implications. It makes the following six recommendations about them.

RECOMMENDATION 28   *In each school system, there should be one or more well-planned instructional materials and resources centers, consisting of* Instructional *at least a library and an audiovisual center. In* materials *each school building, there should also be an* centers *instructional resources facility.*

These centers should be staffed with persons who are adequately prepared in curriculum and instruction, in library service, and in audiovisual education.

There are still schools in the country that either have no library at all or only a meagerly equipped room, called a library, 98 that is inconveniently located, poorly staffed, and little used.

Even when books, equipment, and audio-visual materials are plentiful, their organization and placement may be such that pupils and teachers do not benefit from them to the extent that they might.

Students cannot learn on their own, either in school or later on, without instructional resources or knowledge of how to find and use them. Teachers need source material in order to plan creatively. In view of the wide range of good materials, the variations in frequency of their use, and the expense involved, no one school can hope to provide all these things to all its people all of the time. But every school should be able to draw on these resources as they are needed. The answer lies in division of labor. The Committee believes that the problem can best be met by establishing one or more materials and resources centers in each school system to service a given number of schools. These centers ought to have at least a library and an audiovisual center. In addition, each school ought to have an instructional resources center containing library books and instructional materials that are most constantly in use, plus information on resources which are available elsewhere. The intelligent and efficient use of these aids to learning should be strengthened by a staff that has specialized knowledge in library service and audiovisual education and is conversant with curriculum and teaching methods.

RECOMMENDATION 29 *The use of educational television (ETV) and radio to broaden and deepen learning should be encouraged. Such use should be accompanied by a vigorous program of research and experimentation.*

ETV and radio

The growth of educational television, like that of commercial television, has been spectacular. It has been included in the programs of schools and colleges on a wide scale for total teaching, as in the case of "Continental Classroom"; for course presentation backstopped by the teacher; as a teaching supplement; and for observational purposes to provide students with close-up views, as exemplified by its use in medical and dental schools. ETV has been important, too, for the in-service education of teachers. It has been used to keep parents abreast of their children's learning and experiences in school, particularly in situations where language and cultural differences form a barrier between home and school.

When commercial television burgeoned, the future of radio seemed limited. Actually, radio's role changed but its importance did not decrease. One of the changes was in programming. When much of the entertainment moved over to TV, radio time was freed for coverage of special events and subjects in depth.

Both TV and radio have many important contributions to make to public elementary and secondary education. ETV is still a comparatively young instructional device, but its potentialities are evident. Having survived early exaggerated claims by its enthusiasts and forebodings of doom by its critics, ETV will likely experience a steady and rapid expansion in both quality and quantity in the next decade. The possibilities of radio, a less novel medium, have not been pronounced as dramatically, but they are also clear and merit further exploration.

The validity of ETV and radio as instructional media must continue to be substantiated through research, experimentation, and evaluation. The Committee suggests that schools include ETV and radio in their educational planning as a means of enriching and broadening learning for the student, and that they probe for as yet undiscovered benefits to education.

RECOMMENDATION 30   *Schools should make use, with proper supervision, of self-instructional materials and devices (programed instruction) that facilitate varied learning opportunities and continuous progress for learners of widely divergent abilities. The use of programed instruction should be accompanied by a vigorous program of research and experimentation.*

Programed instruction

There has seldom been an innovation in education that has created as much interest and mushroomed as quickly as programed instruction. Less than ten years ago, not many people in education were familiar with the few experiments conducted on the use of teaching machines for independent learning. Now, the idea has ceased to be bizarre, and many schools and colleges have adopted programed instruction for a number of uses. Reference guides of research literature, experimentation, and available courses programed for machines and in textbooks are out-of-date almost as soon as they are printed. Industry has not only taken up programed instruction in its own training programs, but the production of machines and preparation of texts have become a growth industry itself.

The advantages of devices and materials that will permit an individual to learn efficiently at his own rate, in hours unrelated to a particular schedule, are obvious. These conditions help meet needs for quality education of students with varying abilities and rates of learning, and help to solve the related problems of availability of time and sufficient staff. There are indications that, for certain kinds of learning, programed texts or machines are more efficient than a teacher and that programed learning is retained longer. The implications of programed learning as a means of discovery about the learning process have hardly been touched. Continuing research and experimentation should be fruitful in this regard. A leading theorist and innovator in this field is now exploring the possibility of using machines in teaching certain skills—motor, perceptual, and intellectual—that have until now seemed beyond the reach of explicit teaching methods. The results of his research, if his premise is correct, will be of profound interest to education.

There are two extreme positions about the uses of programed learning. At one extreme is the position that programed learning can lead to individually tailored education; at the other extreme is the position that programed learning can lead to totally standardized education in which the child's every stimulus is determined by a scientific assessment of "the best sequence" and of his aptitudes. Right now educational theory is far over on the side of diversity. Educational practice, however, reflects some standardization at the city or state level, with departures from a plan tolerated. Programed learning can end in the latter extreme. 101

The economics alone may make programed instruction at least as important an innovation as standardized tests were in 1926, for good or evil. Educators will have to be astute to capture the best of the possibilities.

The Committee supports recent advances in programed instruction, provided rational criteria are applied to its use. Questions that might be asked when programed instruction is considered are:

- Does the material available serve educational objectives for the learners concerned? Does it serve these objectives as well as, or better than, other methods?
- What is the ability of the programmer, his knowledge of the subject presented, his knowledge of learning theory?
- Is it preferable for the school to prepare its own programed materials or to use commercially prepared materials?
- What is the quality of the commercial material? Is the presentation valid and appropriate to the task at hand?
- What is the cost? How does cost relate to promise for learning?
- Is another method of presentation more useful?

Careful planning and programming should be prime concerns if the school develops its own materials; quality certainly should be the major consideration if materials are purchased. Many companies are jumping into the field, some for a quick profit, and the materials vary considerably. There is real danger that teaching machines and programed learning will be over-promoted and misused by business *and* education faddists before their real merits and limitations have been properly appraised. It is important, therefore, that the use of programed instruction be accompanied by vigorous research and experimentation.

RECOMMENDATION 31   *A comprehensive study and action program is needed to improve the quality and use of printed teaching materials and other instructional media. Such a study and action program requires the participation of both the producers and the consumers of these instructional materials and media.*

Instructional media

Teaching materials should be high in quality, current in content, and flexible in use. A continuing appraisal of materials of all kinds is needed for good instruction. Such an appraisal is particularly needed in a period characterized by a great expansion of knowledge, including knowledge about people and the ways they learn.

A major problem is that of keeping instructional materials current. New nations emerge, and yesterday's social studies text has a major gap within it. New discoveries are made in science and chemistry, and the textbooks of ten years ago are out of date. During the time it takes to prepare textbooks and films, and it does take time to prepare good ones, there may be many new developments that are pertinent to the subject area under consideration. These changes complicate the production of up-to-date books and films, but if the changes are significant they can not be ignored. And if the customary instructional materials do not keep pace, then provision must be made for supplementing them through other and more current media.

Inadequacies in instructional materials do not always stem simply from the problem of keeping up with rapid change. Some of the inadequacies reflect a lack of sensitivity to changing points of view about what is important to be taught. The very slow shift away from a heavy emphasis on study of Western cultures to adequate consideration of Asian and African cultures is one illustration. The unimaginative retention of certain patterns and placement of content, without sufficient experimentation with other possibilities, is another.

Still another area which needs reappraisal is reading, particularly the content used in the early teaching of reading. Methods of teaching reading have had careful study, and children of today read better than those of yesterday because of the careful research in the teaching of developmental skills. But the purpose of reading is more than acquisition of a skill; it is to provide the student through that skill with information that is important and interesting to him. Books that are dull in style and bland in content, that simplify and repeat maniacally, that portray a very unreal world, do not challenge the student. They can reinforce the uneasy notion that learning is not worth his time and trouble.

The Committee commends recent efforts to upgrade basic readers and to provide students with reading content that has meaning and literary taste. It recommends that these efforts be supplemented by a comprehensive and cooperative study and action program designed to improve the nature and quality of all instructional materials. The producers of instructional materials and the consumers of them are dependent upon each other. The profession needs the best products that publishers and other producers of instructional materials can provide. In turn, producers need from educators a flow of information to guide the development of materials that are educationally sound and financially rewarding.

RECOMMENDATION 32 *School authorities should examine the potentialities of automation for storage and retrieval of pupil personnel data and instruc-*
Automation *tional materials.*

An incredible amount of time is lost to teaching in our schools by the chores of record-keeping, scheduling classes, and keeping track of material that is not in daily use. Even the largest and best-supported schools do not have the clerical staff to help keep up with the amount of detail work that is necessary. The smallest school with the slimmest budget could benefit by being able to allocate to the educational program some of the funds eaten up by nonteaching charges.

Automation of time-consuming expensive practices is not yet as widespread in the educational world as it is in industry, but it should be. School administrators and board members may be apprehensive about initial costs, but this should not dissuade them from exploring the possibilities of automation. Investigation may well disclose real dollar savings later, as well as improved education now.

Some of the data processing systems that are now available include microfilm, punched cards, electronic computers, and
104   punched and electronic tapes. These can be used in various ways,

either within one school, within a district, or in a data-processing center serving several districts on a share-the-cost basis. Some of the tasks that can be taken over by a data processing center are:

- preparing student report cards
- storing cumulative data about each student
- selecting classes and class hours for students on the basis of master class lists
- making master schedules for an entire school
- correcting tests; analyzing test results, preparing test information for teachers and counselors
- gathering and disseminating statistics on the schools

On the last point, the federal government has appropriated funds to help the states plan for improving statistical services by using automatic data processing equipment. All fifty states have approved plans for this purpose, although not all have yet been implemented. The sooner local school districts have these facilities at their disposal, the faster they will have access to pertinent data themselves. They will also be able to provide information about the dimensions of the educational enterprise in America while it is current enough to be useful.

Space
utilization

RECOMMENDATION 33   *New concepts of space should permit and encourage: (a) varying sized groups ranging from small seminars to multiple-class; (b) independent study with visual and/or acoustic privacy as required; (c) access to a variety of instructional media; (d) multiple use.*

Key considerations in planning for better utilization of space are: (a) flexibility, and (b) environment which respects the learner and his need for a sense of amenity if his learning is to be most efficient.

Form follows function. The basic tenet of the revolution in architecture in our generation is nowhere more important than in the design of school buildings. Changes in educational practice and changes in the size and kind of population the school serves modify the function of a school building. Sound planning dictates flexibility in school architecture so that the form of the building permits rather than hampers innovations in the program and remains adaptable to the needs of the community. Educational opportunity *and* money can be frittered away if the relationship between architecture and the processes of education are not observed.

Emphasis on the individual learner, altered concepts of the best use of teacher time, the increased use of educational tools such as television and language laboratories, and programed learning all require re-thinking of the use of space. Modifications needed in vertical and horizontal organization of the school call for the following kinds of space:

- places for reasonably quiet independent study for the individual student
- places for small seminar groups to meet
- standard home-room classes
- large places where sizable numbers of students can gather for lectures and demonstrations
- laboratory-type facilities for many "doing" experiences
- places for teachers to plan and prepare for their classes and to consult privately with individual students

Aesthetic appeal is important, too, not as a frill but to further the ends of the program. Children learn better in a place where they like to be. The school should not be a cheerless, depressing place; it should be an attractive, pleasant environment which encourages children to learn.

Space in existing school facilities can be adapted for some, although not all, of the uses mentioned above. Libraries, cafeterias, and auditoriums that once served only special functions are most readily converted for multiple use. The rigidities in school design in the past, however, make alterations in space utilization difficult, expensive, and sometimes impossible. Most of the new needs of the educational program now can be met only through new construction. The lesson to be learned from the permanence of buildings, coupled with the permanence of change, is to provide for maximum use and flexibility of space at the very beginning.

SUMMARY

Three sets of problems related to planning and organizing for teaching have been discussed in this chapter. They are: organizing the curriculum; organizing the school and classroom; and organizing personnel, space, and materials. Some system of organization is required to give coherence to educational programs. The Committee has pointed out that systems often outlive their usefulness and begin to inhibit rather than enhance educational aims. In its recommendations under the headings listed above, the Committee stressed the need to relate plans to educational objectives and to emphasize flexibility in each area so that change and human variability can be accommodated.

Recommendations in this chapter covered the following topics: curricular sequence, when to teach what, nongraded schools, ability grouping, team teaching, self-contained classroom, classroom grouping, ETV and radio, programed instruction, improved instructional materials, automation, architecture and space use.

Chapter 4

IN THE
FUTURE . . .

Today, as in the past, Americans look to the schools with high expectations—perhaps higher than at any time in our history. Education, always valued, is now more than ever vital to the individual and to the nation. It is the key to many of the social ills in our own society; it is essential in our expanded international involvements. Education is crucial for beginning and continued employment. Expansion of the economy depends on broadly trained leaders as well as on a skilled labor force. In short, the solution of many present-day challenges and problems turns on education—hence, the great public debate on American education and the heightened concern within the profession.

The National Committee of the NEA's Project on Instruction has attempted in this report to make sound and useful recommendations to serve as a guide to the profession and to the public in their combined efforts to improve the instructional program in the schools. The following pages contain a brief review of the general directions the Committee believes desirable for public education in the years ahead.

CLARIFICATION OF ENDS, THE PUBLIC ROLE

Education is so thoroughly meshed into the life and welfare of the nation, the local community, and the family of the pupil that almost everyone has a stake in the schools. Where so many people of diverse opinions and abilities play a variety of roles, the responsibilities peculiar to each participating group is of the utmost importance. Adequate communication among the groups is not only desirable but also vital for the enterprise to move ahead.

American education is based upon a fundamental belief in the ability of the people to make sound decisions about what is best for their children. In our nation, the citizens, acting primarily through their representatives on school boards, determine the broad goals which they expect to achieve through education, indicate these clearly to their elected representatives, and provide the financial support necessary to accomplish the goals they have set. It is important for our citizens to understand and accept these responsibilities.

Many more people are becoming active and vocal in school affairs; yet the challenges that appear on the horizon may require a greater commitment from all of us. This goes beyond getting out the vote on school-board elections and school-bond issues. It involves decisions on educational policies and establishing priorities.

People in a community formulate their educational goals more clearly and make their decisions more wisely when they are informed about the issues, problems, practices, and significant developments in the field of education. They invest their money in education more willingly when they know more about school financing than the cost of a new building. They help keep their children in school more readily when they know more about its program.

Much can be done to help the public enhance its competence in these matters. Educators can be of real service in this regard by explaining what good education is and what it means to a democratic society, by increasing the availability of information, by encouraging public debate, and by providing more learning opportunities in depth for lay citizens.

Educational practice must change, rapidly and profoundly, during the next decade. Such change can come about only with the understanding and encouragement of laymen. The average

American community should maintain a kind of continuous study program on education, open to interested laymen. This should be done through citizens' committees, parent-teacher groups, adult-education programs, and the mass media.

FOCUS ON INTELLECTUAL COMPETENCE

As the pace of change quickens, as technology becomes more specialized, as propaganda and advertising become more subtle, and as international problems become more intricate, the schools will need to give more attention to developing in their students the competence to understand and deal with such complexities.

The ability to think rationally, to use reason and evidence in solving problems and making decisions, extends one's control over the environment. Where immediate control is beyond the individual, the ability to understand and follow the reasoning behind events and confusing issues brings some order to bear on situations in which people may otherwise retreat into apathy or react destructively with blind emotion. The Committee shares with the Educational Policies Commission the view that rational thinking is a central objective of education. In its 1961 report,[26] the Commission said:

> The purpose which runs through and strengthens all other educational purposes—the common thread of education—is the development of the ability to think. This is the central purpose to which the school must be oriented if it is to accomplish either its traditional tasks or those newly accentuated by recent changes in the world. To say that it is central is not to say that it is the sole purpose or in all circumstances the most important purpose, but that it must be a pervasive concern in the work of the school. Many agencies contribute to achieving educational objectives, but this particular objective will not be generally attained unless the school focuses on it. In this context, therefore, the development of every student's rational powers must be recognized as centrally important.

FOCUS ON VOCATIONAL COMPETENCE

An overriding problem for the sixties is unemployment among youth. Already the unemployment rate among people under twenty is between 15 and 20 per cent, roughly three times the national unemployment figure. Yet the number of young people reaching eighteen years of age *each* year will increase from 2.6 million in 1960 to 3.8 million in 1965, a rise of nearly 50 per cent. During the 1960s an estimated 26 million young workers will enter the labor force, or 40 per cent more than in the 1950s.[27]

School officials, working with community and business organizations, are challenged to find new approaches to vocational education. The need for bold and creative programs to meet the needs of *all* children is today one of the most crucial problems, not only of education, but of the nation as well.

Competence in basic understandings and skills is still the best contribution of the elementary schools to future workers, but the schools can also help students learn about the world of work. Depending upon the students and upon associated factors in the community, the public high schools should provide some direct or preparatory vocational experience in some of the following ways:

1. College-bound students need opportunities that provide initial preparation for their life's work. For example, it is becoming increasingly difficult for a student to pursue a collegiate course of study in science and engineering unless he has given special attention to the study of mathematics at the secondary school level.

2. Students who do not plan to continue their formal schooling beyond the secondary level should receive some direct vocational education before graduation. This training should relate to the new industries and skills the economy requires, rather than the outmoded trades perpetuated in some present-day vocational courses.

3. Students among the disadvantaged or culturally deprived need school programs that stress basic skills, relate school experience to work experience and on-the-job training, and help to make up for cultural deficiencies. It is important, however, that these students not be treated intellectually as second-class citizens. The great challenge here is a two-fold one: first, to develop

a program meaningful to these young people, a task which needs much study in depth and which must be tailor-made, in many respects, to each community; second, to relate the school program to employment opportunities.

4. Students who are mentally or physically handicapped should have special opportunities for education.

5. Every secondary school in the United States with a school population of more than 250 to 300 students should have at least one staff member who is competent in vocational guidance, a recommendation made by James B. Conant and seconded here.[28]

American education has been concerned with vocational competence and preparation at least since Benjamin Franklin set up his academy in the mid-eighteenth century. This concern should receive renewed emphasis in the decade ahead as the United States moves further into an urban-industrial society with its demand for increasing specialization, mass production, and more skilled manpower in general. A study of the whole area of vocational education, much of which is outmoded and irrelevant to current needs, is long overdue.

DEVELOPING THE POTENTIALITIES OF THE INDIVIDUAL

The impersonal and mechanistic nature of our mass society makes it more important than ever for the school to have greater concern for the individual—a fact often spoken about, but too infrequently provided for. Renewed emphasis on the individual results from the necessity of providing counter-balance to strong tendencies toward homogenization of tastes and deference to the group.

From the outset the National Committee has made it clear that the educational needs of all youth cannot be met by a single, uniform program of instruction. Throughout our studies there has been continued effort to focus on curriculum developments that provide for each learner.

One series of recommendations, for example, is designed to encourage early identification and preventive programs related to the school dropout, juvenile delinquency, and youth unemployment. There has been concern, too, for issues relative to maximum development of high capacities. Schools should examine the possibilities of work-study programs for some of their students, advanced placement or enrichment programs for others, and should see that school programs offer opportunities for independent study.

Development of creativity is an important aspect of concern for the individual, one that is increasingly significant in educational research. The schools cannot endow students with the creative spark. They can smother it in children who are particularly spontaneous and original, if these qualities are not valued and provided for in the school program.

In research literature on this subject,[29] the creative individual is generally described as intuitive, intelligent (although not all high IQs are creative), intensely curious, capable of tolerating greater disorder and complexity than the average person, and highly independent—a nonconformist at least in the realm of ideas and thinking. All of this adds up to a challenge to the teacher who is free to respond to the special needs and demands of such a child. It spells frustration, discouragement, and sometimes resentment to the teacher who is overworked or uninspired, whose efforts are hampered by an inflexible curriculum, problems of discipline, or chores completely unrelated to teaching.

If schools are to support creativity in the child, they must encourage it in the teacher. Creative teaching means time for the teacher to read and explore, to develop or find new materials, and time to spend with each child in the class. Schools can help make this time available by exploring and experimenting with different ways of freeing the teacher to teach. In a number of schools teacher aides have taken over many tasks that do not require professional skill.

Schools can also encourage creativity in their students by seeing that the schedule is not so rigid or so heavy as to preclude time for children to explore on their own. The degree to which the school itself is willing to engage in exploration and experimentation is a fair gauge of whether it will foster creativity or conformity in its student body.

114

MORE FUNCTIONAL SCHOOL AND CLASSROOM ORGANIZATION

The Committee has recognized that the graded organization of schools may interfere with the continuous, unbroken, upward progression of all learners. Careful consideration of alternative ways of organizing the school vertically, such as multigrading and nongrading, have been recommended in seeking to provide flexible progress plans geared to human variability.

The Committee also has suggested innovations in the horizontal organization of schools and classrooms. Well-planned projects in team teaching appear to offer promise of dealing more effectively with individual differences, using personnel resources more effectively, and challenging teachers with differing interests and talents. Whatever specific form of horizontal organization is adopted in a local school, the Committee has advocated adequate provision of a close counseling relationship of each pupil with teachers who know him well.

The organization of class groups has been as controversial an issue in the Committee's deliberations as it has been elsewhere. The Committee has recognized that homogeneous interclass grouping might be employed to meet the diverse needs of individuals provided that many criteria are considered in setting up such groups. Those concerned, however, must realize that grouping on the basis of student ability or achievement, without accompanying curricular and instructional provisions, does not assure increased academic achievement and probably restrains some other important learning. Within the classroom, learners should be organized frequently into smaller groups of varying sizes for more ease of involvement of each individual in the various learning tasks. The size and membership of these instructional groups will vary according to the purpose and nature of the learning activity.

TOWARD EFECTIVE USE OF TIME, SPACE, AND INSTRUCTIONAL RESOURCES

There has been much concern about the impact of technology on our lives and the consequent, often sudden, disappearance from the scene of many things which, at their passing, are all the more valued. Nostalgia for more simple and serene times crops up often. At the same time, most people are eager for the fruits of the new technology and readily adopt their use in industry and at home.

Education cannot muddle through in the traditional setting in the traditional way while the rest of society promptly employs new technical resources and reorganizes whole industries on the basis of their use. Fortunately, the press for efficiency, variety, and aesthetics in school design and for the use of technology at appropriate points in the school program is well begun.

In both new and old buildings, technological developments, such as TV, tape-recordings, teaching machines, language laboratories, films and filmstrips, already have made marked contributions to the curriculum. Their use is expected to spread widely in the future. Computers have been tried in the complicated task of developing a master schedule, where pupils' and teachers' time, course offerings, and classroom space somehow have to be matched and made to come out even.

A number of schools have already been built that architecturally reflect the best current knowledge about learning and aids to learning. The designs stress flexibility and amenity in the school environment. A new demonstration school being developed by the New York University School of Education and the architect, I. M. Pei, will, it is hoped, solve some big-city school problems of high land costs by building upward and distributing the playground site into, under, and on top of the building. Harold Gores describes this effort to provide city school children with more refreshing surroundings: [30]

> It is quite possible that some day this building in its high-rise setting will be literally alive from top to bottom with the shrubs and flowers the children planted. A sunflower, though eighty feet in the air, is still a sunflower, and the big city could use a few to diminish its brassy, glassy facelessness.

The tremendous potential of new instructional materials and technology has been recognized in the Committee's recommendations on the use of educational television and radio, programed

116

learning, instructional materials centers, and automation. Schools interested in exploring the possibilities will find much experience and information at their disposal from such sources as the Educational Facilities Laboratory, the Center for Programed Instruction, and the many school systems that are experimenting with television classes on a wide scale. The most exciting designs and the best uses of new media are yet to come, however, and this should be an·interesting era in space-and-materials planning in education.

Gores[31] gives an interesting progression in educational emphases that underlie new concepts of space:

FROM	TO
1. The group	The individual
2. Memory	Inquiry
3. Spiritless climate	Zest for learning
4. The graded school	The nongraded school
5. Self-contained classroom	Self-contained school
6. Scheduled classes	Appointments and independent learning
7. Teacher as general practitioner	Teacher as clinical specialist (member of team)
8. School building use geared to an agrarian society — nine-month year—limited to children	School building use reflecting urban society—twelve-month year—available to all age groups
9. Classrooms that are like kitchens	Classrooms that are like libraries, living rooms
10. Boxes and egg crates	Clusters and zones of space
11. Teaching as telling	Teaching as guiding
12. A teaching schedule of 30 hours a week with children in class and 15 hours for planning and correcting	15 hours a week with children in class and 30 hours for research, planning, and development

RESEARCH, EXPERIMENTATION, AND INNOVATION

Whether it consists of a few schools or several hundred, the local school system is the key to educational progress. However much it may be aided and stimulated by university research centers, state departments of education, national and state education associations, and national curriculum projects, the local school system must have energy, interest, and initiative if it is to change for the better. Participation in educational experiments creates excitement, momentum, and change, as can be seen in the schools associated with the many new curriculum projects now under way. Teaching is poorest when the teacher is not interested. We need a thousand *experimental schools,* each with a corps of enthusiastic and interested teachers, supervisors, and administrators at work on projects they have selected and designed themselves. Should not educational experiment stations, somewhat like agricultural experiment stations, dot our land?

A school or school system can start the process of curriculum improvement any time, any place, without a long period of survey and planning. It can identify areas of the curriculum where teachers are ready to initiate changes and move forward in these areas. One school with a group of interested teachers and a supervisor may reconstruct its mathematics program, another school work on science, and still another on foreign language at the elementary-school level. One high-school faculty may work on social studies and history, another may develop a system of senior honors courses in English, mathematics, science, and social science. A school system can set up a study group on dropouts and culturally deprived children and within a few months launch an experimental program based on its study.

A comprehensive study of the entire instructional program of a school system, from kindergarten through grade twelve in all content areas, is recommended at periodic intervals. To accomplish all of these ends it is essential that we strive for a teaching load for public school teachers comparable to that of their colleagues in higher education. If teachers are to keep abreast of the content they teach and the innovations in education, time for thinking and planning needs to be made available.

School systems in large cities and counties should maintain their own research staffs for work on research, experimentation, and innovation. These staffs can profit from close cooperation with state departments of education, state education associations, and university research groups. Small school systems should band together so their research funds are spent wisely. The National Committee has recommended that each school system allocate a definite and adequate proportion—at least one per cent—of its annual operating budget for the support of research, planning, and development.

Every state department of education and every state education association needs a research and evaluation staff to work on state-wide and local-school curriculum programs. This work is in addition to the regular collection and analysis of educational data.

Major centers for research and development in curriculum and instruction should be established in the various geographical regions of the country. There should be at least four major centers, amply supported with research funds from private and public sources, designed to prepare personnel for research work in universities, state and federal departments of education, state and national organizations, and local school systems.

A National Center for the Study of Curriculum and Instruction should be established to give leadership to the schools of the nation as they seek to pursue excellence. Scholars in residence at the Center, a panel of consultants across the country attached to various universities and other educational institutions and organizations, graduate interns and fellows, a Clearing House, a National Commission on Priorities in Education—these are some of the essential resources needed to provide leadership and support of change.

GUIDELINES FOR A SCHOOL SYSTEM'S SELF-STUDY

Continuous reference has been made to the necessity for each school system to survey its own house before attempting to put it in order. None of the recommendations by this or any other national committee concerned with advancement and improvement of education is of any import unless it is adapted for and adopted by the local schools. Nor will any changes be effective if they are tacked on to an already creaky and lumbering program.

Postponement of a survey of part or all of a school system's program is the most natural thing in the world. Teachers, like the old woman in the shoe, have so many children they don't know what to do; administrators stretch their work days into nights to keep up with the demands of their daily schedule. Finding the time for school personnel to devote to study of their school is often the hardest part of the task. If the effort is made, however, it can be most rewarding and revitalizing for the people involved and for the school as a whole. It is strongly urged that school people consider a self-study as the first step in freeing time and energies, now taken up by marginally effective practices, for more creative planning and teaching.

The twelve questions cited below, which served as the base for the Committee's work, are restated here to serve as guidelines for use by professional staff members of a school system in assessing the status and needs of its instructional program. Undoubtedly some will be found more appropriate than others, and entirely new questions will arise as the local situation dictates special inquiry in one direction or another. These are a beginning:

1. Who should make what decisions about education?
2. How can an extensive program of educational research, experimentation, and innovation be developed?
3. How can the instructional program of the school be designed to develop the individual potentialities of all members of the school population within the framework of a society that values both unity and diversity?
4. What are the distinctive responsibilities of the school in contrast to those that are distinctive to the family, the church, industry, and various youth-serving agencies? What responsibilities should the school share with other institutions and with other youth-serving agencies? What, then, should be included in the school program? What should be excluded from it?

5. What is the school's role in dealing with serious national

problems such as youth unemployment and juvenile delinquency?

6. What is the school's role in teaching about controversial issues and about communism and other ideologies?

7. How can the school provide a balanced program for the individual and maintain it amidst various pressures for specialization?

8. How can schools make wise selections of content from the ever-growing body of available knowledge?

9. How should the content of the curriculum be organized?

10. How should the curriculum of the school be organized to give appropriate direction to the instructional process?

11. How should the school and the classroom be organized to make the most effective use of the time and talents of students and teachers?

12. How can the quality of instructional materials be improved? How can the products of modern technology be used effectively? How can space be designed and used to support the instructional program?

IN CONCLUSION

The *right* questions are those questions which lead to thoughtful consideration of facts that are pertinent to the intelligent solution of educational problems. But even as educators and laymen are arriving at decisions on issues in education at any given period, some of the *right* questions and some of the key issues are changing. Only by a continuing quest for knowledge and by awareness of shifts and changes in the determining conditions of education can its leaders be responsive to the needs of the individual and of society. There is no better way for teachers and students to become acquainted with the fact of change, the value of analyzing the problems involved in change, and the positive response to change than through cooperative planning and willingness to meet new challenges.

To move our reports from bookshelves to action requires joint effort that reflects the creative intelligence of all of us, from the national to the local levels, from every range of interest and opinion. The iconoclasts can challenge tradition; the conservatives can insist that innovations be validated; parents can demand high quality and contribute to its realization. Change there will be. Nothing remains static for long. But with effort and imagination the forthcoming changes in education can culminate in new heights of excellence. We urge our colleagues and the public to join in the task.

Recommendations of the National Committee of the NEA Project on Instruction (A Summary List)

DECISION AREA I Decision-Making

Who should make what decisions about education?

Local school boards

RECOMMENDATION 1 *Local school boards are the legal instruments through which the state fulfills its responsibility for education. The distinction between lay control of school policies determined by the board of education and implementation of these policies by the professional staff, with the leadership of the local superintendent, should be delineated, understood, and respected.*

Federal government

RECOMMENDATION 2 *The federal government should provide the types of assistance needed to improve local and state systems of education. Two types of federal assistance should be stressed: (a) the federal government should provide general financial assistance for the improvement of public education; (b) the U.S. Office of Education should have an expanded role in stimulating experimentation and innovation in the schools, in providing statistical analyses of importance, and in disseminating information about educational problems and promising practices.*

123

RECOMMENDATION 3 *Local school faculties should have the freedom and the authority to make decisions about what to teach—within state and local requirements—and how to teach. Final instructional decisions should be made by the teacher, taking into consideration recommendations from appropriate local, state, and national groups representing the teaching profession, academic scholars, and the public.*

Local school faculties

RECOMMENDATION 4 *State educational authorities should establish standards for public school instruction, provide adequate resources for their achievement, and give dynamic leadership to curriculum development, experimentation, and innovation in local schools.*

State educational authorities

RECOMMENDATION 5 *State legislatures should set forth general goals for the schools, provide adequate financial support, and delegate broad powers of implementation to the state and local educational authorities. The state legislature should not prescribe curriculum content or legislate specific courses.*

State legislatures

DECISION AREA II Research, Experimentation, and Innovation

How can an extensive program of educational research, experimentation, and innovation be developed?

RECOMMENDATION 6. *School systems should allocate an appropriate proportion of their annual operating budgets—not less than 1 per cent—for the support of research, experimentation, and innovation.*

Money, time, and personnel

Adequate time should be provided for each

staff member to participate in curriculum planning, research, evaluation, and other activities designed to improve the instructional program.

RECOMMENDATION 7   *Adequately staffed and supported regional curriculum and instruction centers should be encouraged. These centers, located mainly in universities, should work in partnership with local schools to initiate innovation and conduct experimentation and research to improve the instructional program of the public schools.*

Regional curriculum and instruction centers

RECOMMENDATION 8   *Efforts of nationally oriented, nongovernmental groups to stimulate curricular and instructional experimentation and innovation should be encouraged. Scholars in the academic fields and the teaching profession should be involved in such efforts.*

Nongovernmental groups

DECISION AREA III   Educating All Children and Youth*

How can the instructional program of the school be designed to develop the individual potentialities of all members of the school population within the framework of a society that values both unity and diversity?

RECOMMENDATION 9   *The instructional program should provide: (a) opportunities for developing the individual potentialities represented in the wide range of differences among people; (b) a common fund of knowledge, values, and skills vital to the welfare of the individual and the nation.*

The individual and the nation

To achieve these objectives, the instructional program cannot be the same for all. Provision for individual differences should be made by qualified

---

* Decision Areas III through IX, including Recommendations 9 through 19, are related to "Deciding What To Teach."

*teaching personnel through diagnosis of learning
needs and through appropriate variety of content,
resources for learning, and instructional methods.*

What are the distinctive responsibilities of the school in contrast
to those that are distinctive to the family, the church, industry,
and various youth-serving agencies?

What responsibilities should the school share with other institutions and with other youth-serving agencies?

What, then, should be included in the school program?

What should be excluded from it?

RECOMMENDATION 10   *Priorities for the school
are the teaching of skills in reading, composition,
listening, speaking (both native and foreign languages), and computation . . . ways of creative and
disciplined thinking, including methods of inquiry
and application of knowledge . . . competence in
self-instruction and independent learning . . . fundamental understanding of the humanities and the
arts, the social sciences and natural sciences, and
mathematics . . . appreciation of and discriminating
taste in literature, music, and the visual arts . . . instruction in health education and physical education.*

*Distinctive
and shared
responsibilities*

*Responsibilities best met by joint efforts of the
school and other social agencies include: development of values and ideals . . . social and civic competence . . . vocational preparation.*

*The decision to include or exclude particular
school subjects or outside-of-class activities should
be based on: (a) the priorities assigned to the
school and to other agencies; (b) data about*

126

learners and society, and developments in the academic disciplines; (c) the human and material resources available in the school and community.

DECISION AREA V   The School's Role in Dealing with National Problems Related to Youth

What is the school's role in dealing with serious national problems such as youth unemployment and juvenile delinquency?

Youth unemployment and juvenile delinquency

RECOMMENDATION 11   *The schools can help to combat such serious national problems as youth unemployment and juvenile delinquency by: (a) evaluating the intellectual and creative potential of all children and youth in the schools; (b) identifying early the potential dropout and delinquent; (c) developing positive programs to challenge these young people to educational endeavor; (d) participating in cooperative programs with parents and with community groups and organizations— business and industry, labor, service groups, government agencies, and the many youth-serving agencies*

DECISION AREA VI   Teaching About Controversial Issues and About Communism

What is the school's role in teaching about controversial issues and about communism and other ideologies?

Controversial issues

RECOMMENDATION 12   *Rational discussion of controversial issues should be an important part of the school program. The teacher should help students identify relevant information, learn the techniques of critical analysis, make independent judg-*

127

ments, and be prepared to present and support them. The teacher should also help students become sensitive to the continuing need for objective re-examination of issues in the light of new information and changing conditions in society.

RECOMMENDATION 13   To help the student think critically about current issues, the curriculum should provide opportunities for adequate instruction concerning social forces and trends. Attention commensurate with their significance in modern society should be given to issues such as international relations, economic growth, urbanization, population growth, science and technology, and mass media.

Current social forces and trends

RECOMMENDATION 14   The school curriculum should include a study of political and social ideologies focusing upon communism. The methods of rational inquiry should be stressed. The study should be set in the perspective of the modern world and be incorporated into the instructional program at appropriate points. If a special unit on communism is deemed desirable in the secondary school, it should supplement and complement earlier study of these topics.

Teaching about communism

As with other areas of the curriculum, decisions about what to teach and how to teach about these topics should be based upon policies developed by school administrators and teachers of the local school system. In the formulation and implementation of such policies, school personnel should utilize the resources of scholarship and be supported in their decisions by the school board and by an informed community opinion.

How can the school provide a balanced program for the individual and maintain it amidst various pressures for specialization?

Ways of achieving balance

RECOMMENDATION 15   *The school can provide and maintain a curriculum appropriately balanced for each student by offering a comprehensive program of studies, making early and continuous assessment of individual potentialities and achievements, and providing individualized programs based on careful counseling.*

To avoid the imbalance that can result from limiting financial support to certain selected subjects and services, general financial support should be provided for the total program. This applies to local, state, and federal support.

How can schools make wise selections of content from the ever-growing body of available knowledge?

Bases for selecting content

RECOMMENDATION 16   *The objectives of the school, with a clear statement of priorities, should give direction to all curriculum planning. This applies to adding content, eliminating content, or changing the emphases on various topics and fields of study.*

Keeping content up-to-date

RECOMMENDATION 17   *Each curriculum area should be under continuous study and evaluation and should be reviewed periodically. One purpose of such reviews is to determine whether recent findings in the academic disciplines are, or should be, reflected in the instructional program. These reviews should utilize the knowledge and skills of*

129

the teacher, the school administrator, the scholar in the academic disciplines, the scholar in the profession of teaching, and the lay citizen, each contributing his special competence to the total task.

RECOMMENDATION 18   *In making selections of content, school staffs should study the results and recommendations of curriculum projects sponsored by nationally oriented groups with a view to applying promising findings.*

National curriculum projects

There should be a systematic procedure for studying the results of these curriculum projects. The procedure should recognize the importance of balance and continuity in the total school experience of students and include the steps prerequisite to curriculum changes.

DECISION AREA IX   Organizing Content

How should the content of the curriculum be organized?

RECOMMENDATION 19   *The content of the curriculum should be organized in such ways that students may progress, from early to later school years, toward an increasingly mature utilization and organization of their knowledge. Helping learners see interrelationships and achieve unity from the diversity of knowledge is basic to any organization of content.*

Bases for organizing content

School staffs should experiment with a variety of ways of organizing content. The nature, meaning, and structure of the discipline and differences in the ways students learn should be taken into account in selecting a particular plan of organization and evaluating its effectiveness.

130

DECISION AREA X   Organizing the Curriculum*

How should the curriculum of the school be organized to give appropriate direction to the instructional process?

Educational objectives

RECOMMENDATION 20   *The aims of education should serve as a guide for making decisions about curriculum organization as well as about all other aspects of the instructional program.*

The public, through the local school board, is responsible for determining the broad aims of education. The professional staff is responsible for translating the broad aims into specific objectives that indicate priorities and define clearly the behaviors intended for the learners. The local board of education has responsibility for seeing that an acceptable statement of objectives and priorities is prepared and for endorsing such a statement.

Curricular sequence

RECOMMENDATION 21   *In each curricular area, the vertical organization of subject matter should take account of: (a) the logical structure of the subject; (b) the difficulty of material as related to the student's intellectual maturity; (c) the relation of the field to other fields.*

Procedures and instruments for evaluating pupil progress must be specifically geared to the school's educational goals and to the curricular sequence in use in the school.

When to teach what

RECOMMENDATION 22   *The fact that very young children can learn relatively difficult aspects of science, mathematics, and other subjects is at best an incomplete answer to the question of whether they should learn them at this particular*

---

* Decision Areas X through XII, including Recommendations 20 through 33, are related to "Planning and Organizing for Teaching."

stage of their development. Decisions about when to teach what should be based on both the learner's ability to understand and the relative importance of alternative ways of using the learner's time at any given point in his school experience.

DECISION AREA XI   Organizing the School and
the Classroom

How should the school and the classroom be organized to make the most effective use of the time and talents of students and teachers?

RECOMMENDATION 23   *The vertical organization of the school should provide for the continuous, unbroken, upward progression of all learners, with due recognition of the wide variability among learners in every aspect of their development. The school organization should, therefore, provide for differentiated rates and means of progression toward achievement of educational goals.*

Nongrading, multigrading, grading

Nongrading and multigrading are promising alternatives to the traditional graded school and should be given careful consideration in seeking to provide flexible progress plans geared to human variability.

RECOMMENDATION 24   *The assignment of pupils to classroom groups should be based on knowledge about students and teachers and on understanding of goals to be achieved.*

Bases for ability grouping

Efforts to set up groups in terms of ability and/or achievement do little to reduce the over-all range of pupil variability with which teachers must deal. However, selective grouping and regrouping by

132

achievement sometimes is useful, particularly at the secondary-school level.

RECOMMENDATION 25   *In order to provide individually planned programs for learners, taking into account the specific objectives to be achieved, the horizontal organization of the school should permit flexibility in assigning pupils to instructional groups that may range in size from one pupil to as many as a hundred or more. Well-planned cooperative efforts among teachers—efforts such as team teaching, for example—should be encouraged and tested.*

Team teaching

RECOMMENDATION 26   *The school should be organized in such a way that it provides opportunity for each student to: (a) experience continuity and relatedness in his learning, and (b) have a close counseling relationship with competent teachers who know him well. Various forms of organization should be explored to determine their effectiveness for these purposes.*

Self-contained classroom

The contributions of specialized personnel should be used as students progress through the elementary and secondary school. At whatever point specialized personnel are brought into the instructional program, their work should be coordinated with and related to the total program.

RECOMMENDATION 27   *In schools where the classroom is the unit of organization, teachers should organize learners frequently into smaller groups of varying types and sizes. Decisions as to size and membership of such groups should be based on knowledge about learners and on the specific educational purposes to be served at a given time for each learner.*

Classroom grouping

133

How can the quality of instructional materials be improved? How can the products of modern technology be used effectively? How can space be designed and used to support the instructional program?

Instructional materials centers

RECOMMENDATION 28   *In each school system, there should be one or more well-planned instructional materials and resources centers, consisting of at least a library and an audiovisual center. In each school building, there should also be an instructional resources facility.*

These centers should be staffed by persons who are adequately prepared in curriculum and instruction, in library service, and in audiovisual education.

ETV and radio

RECOMMENDATION 29   *The use of educational television (ETV) and radio to broaden and deepen learning should be encouraged. Such use should be accompanied by a vigorous program of research and experimentation.*

Programed instruction

RECOMMENDATION 30   *Schools should make use, with proper supervision, of self-instructional materials and devices (programed instruction) that facilitate varied learning opportunities and continuous progress for learners of widely divergent abilities. The use of programed instruction should be accompanied by a vigorous program of research and experimentation.*

Instructional media

RECOMMENDATION 31   *A comprehensive study and action program is needed to improve the quality and use of printed teaching materials and other instructional media. Such a study and action program requires the participation of both the pro-*

134

ducers and the consumers of these instructional materials and media.

RECOMMENDATION 32 *School authorities should examine the potentialities of automation for storage and retrieval of pupil personnel data and instructional materials.*

Automation

RECOMMENDATION 33 *New concepts of space should permit and encourage: (a) varying sized groups ranging from small seminars to multiple-class; (b) independent study with visual and/or acoustic privacy as required; (c) access to a variety of instructional media; (d) multiple use.*

Space utilization

Key considerations in planning for better utilization of space are: (a) flexibility, and (b) environment which respects the learner and his need for a sense of amenity if his learning is to be most efficient.

135

APPENDIX B

Footnotes

1. McGill, Ralph, "Education: The Key to the Future." Copyright by The Hall Syndicate, Inc. Reprinted by permission.

2. Major reports of the Project on Instruction supporting this volume are:
   Deciding What To Teach. Washington, D.C.: National Education Association, 1963.
   Education in a Changing Society. Washington, D.C.: National Education Association, 1963.
   Planning and Organizing for Teaching. Washington, D.C.: National Education Association, 1963.

3. Goodlad, John I., *Some Propositions in Search of Schools.* Washington, D.C.: Department of Elementary School Principals, National Education Association, 1962, p. 1.

4. For ideas in this section, the Committee has drawn upon the writings of Jerome S. Bruner, Lee J. Cronbach, Robert J. Havighurst, Philip H. Phenix, Joseph J. Schwab, and Ralph W. Tyler. In addition, two of the Project auxiliary reports have been used:
   The Scholars Look at the Schools: A Report of the Disciplines Seminar. Washington, D.C.: National Education Association, February, 1962, 64 p.
   The Principals Look at the Schools: A Status Study of Selected Instructional Practices. Washington, D.C.: National Education Association, April, 1962, 76 p.

5. *Education in a Changing Society, op. cit.*

6. These ideas are drawn from an unpublished letter by Lee J. Cronbach, Professor of Educational Psychology, University of Illinois.

7. Tyler, Ralph W., "Emphasize Tasks Appropriate for the School," *Phi Delta Kappan* 40:73–74, November, 1958.

8. Schreiber, Daniel, "School Dropouts," *NEA Journal* 51:51–52, May, 1962.

9. Brackenbury, Robert L., "A Case for Controversy," *The National Elementary Principal* 42:18, April, 1963.

10. Copyright by the *New York Times,* June 2, 1963. Reprinted by permission.

11. Fraser, Dorothy M., *Current Curriculum Studies in Academic Subjects.* Washington, D.C.: National Education Association, June, 1962, 101 p.

12. *The Washington Post,* January 21, 1963.

13. Schwab, Joseph J., "Education and the Structure of the Disciplines." Unpublished working paper prepared for the NEA Project on Instruction. September 1961, 67 pp.

14. *Ibid.*

15. *Ibid.*

16. Fraser, *op. cit.*

17. *The Principals Look at the Schools: A Status Study of Selected Instructional Practices, op. cit.*

18. *Roles, Responsibilities, Relationships of the School Board, Superintendent, and Staff.* Washington, D.C.: American Association of School Administrators, 1963, p. 4.

19. *The Scholars Look at the Schools: A Report of the Disciplines Seminar, op. cit.*

20. Goodlad, John I., and Rehage, Kenneth, "Unscrambling the Vocabulary of School Organization," *NEA Journal* 51:34–36, November, 1962.

21. Ayres, Leonard P., *Laggards in Our Schools.* New York: Charities Publication Committee, 1909.

22. Goodlad, John I., and Anderson, Robert H., *The Nongraded Elementary School.* New York: Harcourt, Brace and World, 1963, p. 18.

23. Otto, Henry J. "Elementary Education—III, Organization and Administration" in W. S. Monroe, (ed.), *Encyclopedia of Educational Research.* Rev. ed. New York: Macmillan Co., 1950, p. 377–78.

24. Trump, J. Lloyd, and Baynham, Dorsey, *Focus on Change.* Chicago: Rand McNally & Company, 1961, p. 32.

25. *Ibid.*

26. *The Central Purpose of American Education.* Washington, D.C.: Educational Policies Commission, National Education Association, 1961, p. 12.

27. U. S. Department of Labor, *Manpower Challenge of the 1960's.* Washington, D.C.: Government Printing Office, 1960, p. 4, 14.

28. Conant, James B., *The American High School Today.* New York: McGraw-Hill Book Co., 1959, p. 44.

29. Getzels, Jacob W., and Jackson, Philip W., *Creativity and Intelligence.* New York: John Wiley & Sons, Inc., 1962.

30. Gores, Harold B., "The Big Change." An address delivered to the 43rd Annual Convention of the New York State School Boards Association, December, 1962.

31. *Ibid.*

APPENDIX C

Officials of the National Education Association, the National Committee, and Others Involved in This Volume

NEA Officials

Robert Wyatt
William G. Carr
Lyle W. Ashby
Lawrence G. Derthick

President*
Executive Secretary
Deputy Executive Secretary
Assistant Executive Secretary for Educational Services

* The NEA presidents in office during the life of the Project were: Hazel A. Blanchard, Ewald Turner, and Clarice Kline.

National Committee

Melvin W. Barnes, Chairman
Superintendent of Schools
Portland, Oregon

Thomas G. Pullen, Jr.
Vice-Chairman
State Superintendent of Schools
Baltimore, Maryland

William M. Alexander
Professor of Education
George Peabody College for
    Teachers

Sarah C. Caldwell
Teacher, Kent Junior High School
Akron, Ohio

Hollis L. Caswell
President Emeritus
Teachers College
Columbia University

Joe A. Chandler
Executive Secretary
Washington Education Association

Rufus E. Clement
President
Atlanta University

Marion Cranmore
Principal, Burns Park School
Ann Arbor, Michigan

Carol Douglass
College of Education
University of South Florida

Robert J. Havighurst
Professor of Education
University of Chicago

James D. Logsdon
Superintendent
Thornton Township High Schools
and Junior College
Harvey, Illinois

Project Staff

Director
Ole Sand

Associate Director
Richard I. Miller

Program Specialist
Margery Thompson

Philip H. Phenix
Professor of Education
Teachers College
Columbia University

I. James Quillen, Dean
School of Education
Stanford University

G. Baker Thompson
Superintendent
Delaware County
Media, Pennsylvania

Staff Assistants

Therese Fleishman
Marjorie Glenton
Margaret Overington

Committee Reports

In addition to members of the National Committee, each of whom took responsibility for officially reviewing one volume, other persons served as writers and members of Reviewing Committees for this volume and for the three supporting Project publications.

Volume I. *Schools for the Sixties*

Writers: Robert J. Havighurst
Professor of Education
University of Chicago

Dorothy Neubauer
Associate Executive
Secretary
Department of Elementary
School Principals, NEA

Margery Thompson
Program Specialist
NEA Project on Instruction

Ole Sand, Director
NEA Project on Instruction

Richard I. Miller
Associate Director
NEA Project on Instruction

Volume II. Deciding What To Teach

Writer: Dorothy M. Fraser
Professor of Education
Hunter College
City University of New York

Volume III. Education in a Changing Society

Writer: Richard I. Miller
Associate Director
NEA Project on Instruction

Volume IV. Planning and Organizing for Teaching

Writer: John I. Goodlad
Professor of Education
University of California, Los Angeles

Unpublished Position Papers—Writers of

Cook, Lloyd Allen. "Questions about, Comments on, and Extensions of the Fraser and Goodlad Outlines." June, 1961, 43 pp.

"Human Development Principles Offered for Consideration in the Preparation of Materials on 'What To Teach' and 'Organizing for Instruction,'" prepared by a Staff Committee, Institute for Child Study, University of Maryland, July, 1961, 39 pp.

Schwab, Joseph J. "Education and the Structure of the Disciplines." September, 1961, 67 pp.

Stephens, J. M. "Suggestions from the Psychology of Learning." July, 1961, 35 pp.

Eboch, Sidney E. "Space, Time, and Instructional Resources." March, 1963, 14 pp.

Participants in Disciplines Seminar

Ralph W. Tyler, Chairman

George B. Carson

Stanley Chapple

Lee J. Cronbach

David Easton

Gilbert C. Finlay

Alfred B. Garrett

George Gerbner

Preston E. James

Albert H. Marckwardt

William Riley Parker

Philip H. Phenix

G. Baley Price

I. James Quillen

B. Othanel Smith

Joseph J. Schwab

Lawrence Senesh

Gresham M. Sykes

Frederick J. Whiteman

Participant-Observers in Disciplines Seminar

Melvin W. Barnes, Arno A. Bellack, Howard R. Boozer, Sarah C. Caldwell, Philip J. Conley, Marion Cranmore, Howard H. Cummings, George W. Denemark, Dorothy M. Fraser, John I. Goodlad, Paul R. Hanna, William C. Hartshorn, Robert E. Henze, Frederick H. Jackson, J. Boyer Jarvis, Philip Lambert, Rose Lammel, John R. Mayor, Willard C. Olson, Thomas G. Pullen, Jr., I. James Quillen, Henry W. Riecken, Robert M. Rosenzweig, Boyd C. Shafer, Robert L. Silber, B. Othanel Smith, Mortimer Smith, John M. Stephens, Florence Stratemeyer, Fred R. Thompson, Gordon B. Turner, Richard H. Wilson, F. L. Wormald.

Participants in Seminar on Social Forces and Trends

Ralph W. Tyler, Chairman

Lee Benson

Moe L. Frankel

Ralph H. Gabriel

Morris Janowitz

Harold D. Lasswell

Dorothy Lee

Hans Morgenthau

Vincent Ostrom

Joseph J. Schwab

Harold Taylor

William Van Til

J. Russell Wiggins

Howard Wilson

Dael Wolfle

143

Others Who Assisted in the Preparation and Review of This Volume

Literally thousands of people have helped at various stages in the preparation of this report. The contribution of each individual is deeply appreciated although space does not permit the listing of every name. Below are the names of persons who have given special help in the preparation of *Schools for the Sixties.*

George E. Arnstein, Dorsey Baynham, Arno E. Bellack, Vista E. Bishop, Hazel Blanchard, Bertha P. Boyd, Robert L. Brackenbury, Marge Bruce, Ross M. Coxe, Hazel Davis, Nelda Davis, Mary Dawson, Barbara Dickinson, Sidney Dorros, Elizabeth Doucarellis, Roy Edelfeldt, Marion Edman, Henry Ehlers, Donald P. Ely, Frank Estvan, James D. Finn, Arthur W. Foshay, Roy O. Frantz, Margaret Gill, Harold Gores, Glen Heathers, Helen Heffernan, Frank W. Hubbard, Bernard Kaplan, Sam M. Lambert, Rose Lammel, Dorris M. Lee, Gertrude Lewis, Robert M. McClure, James McDonald, Philip E. McPherson, Edward J. Meade, Jr., John Michaelis, Alice Miel, Mrs. Delmas Miller, Corma A. Mowrey, Helen Olson, Don Orton, J. Cecil Parker, Glen E. Robinson, James E. Russell, William Saltonstall, Esther Schroeder, Elena M. Sliepcevich, Glenn E. Snow, Sue Spain, James Squire, Edna Sterling, Esther J. Swenson, J. Lloyd Trump, Ewald Turner, Louise Tyler, William Van Til, Allan West, Fred Wilhelms, Ethel Yari.

APPENDIX D

Reports of the NEA Project on Instruction

Major Reports

Schools for the Sixties: A Report of the NEA Project on Instruction. New York: McGraw-Hill Book Company, Inc., 1963.

Deciding What To Teach. Washington, D.C.: National Education Association, 1963.

Education in a Changing Society. Washington, D.C.: National Education Association, 1963.

Planning and Organizing for Teaching. Washington, D.C.: National Education Association, 1963.

Auxiliary Reports

The Scholars Look at the Schools: A Report of the Disciplines Seminar. Washington, D.C.: National Education Association, February, 1962, 64 p.

The Principals Look at the Schools: A Status Study of Selected Instructional Practices. Washington, D.C.: National Education Association, April, 1962, 76 p.

Current Curriculum Studies in Academic Subjects, by Dorothy M. Fraser. Washington, D.C.: National Education Association, June, 1962, 101 p.

Articles in Periodicals

Alexander, William M.: "Assessing Curriculum Proposals," *Teachers College Record* 63:286–293, January, 1962.

Barnes, Melvin W.: "Developments in Instruction," *Educational Leadership* 20:261–265, January, 1963.

Fraser, Dorothy M.: "What Content and When?" *The National Elementary Principal* 42:13–19, September, 1962.

Goodlad, John I.: "Toward Improved School Organization." *Elementary School Organization.* Fortieth Yearbook. Washington, D.C.: 145

Articles in Periodicals

Department of Elementary School Principals, National Education Association, 1961, Chapter 4, pp. 60–127.

Hanna, Paul R.: "Curriculum and Instruction," *NEA Journal* 52:52–54, January, 1963.

Havighurst, Robert J., and Alexander, William M.: "Bases for Curriculum Decisions," *The National Elementary Principal* 42:8–12, September, 1962.

Miller, Richard I.: "Teaching About Communism in the Public Schools," *Journal of Secondary Education* 38:198–210, April, 1963.

———: "Curriculum Frontiers in the 60's," *Illinois School Board Journal* 30:17–18, 21, 25, March–April, 1963.

———: "Teaching About Communism," *The Saturday Review* 46:62–64, 76–78, March 23, 1963.

———: "Science and Values," *The Science Teacher* 29:5, December, 1962.

Pullen, Thomas G., and Fraser, Dorothy M.: "What To Teach?" *NEA Journal* 51:34–36, October, 1962.

Rehage, Kenneth, and Goodlad, John I.: "Unscrambling the Vocabulary of School Organization," *NEA Journal* 51:34–36, November, 1962.

Sand, Ole: "Six Basic Issues in Determining What To Teach," *Chicago Schools Journal* 43:170–177; January, 1962.

———: "The Profession Speaks: NEA Project on Instruction," *NEA Journal* 50:53–54, May, 1961.

———: "Reports on Some National Studies in Education: The NEA Project on Instruction." *The Bulletin of the National Association of Secondary School Principals* 47:163–170, April, 1963.

———: "The Instructional Program of the Public Schools," *Leadership Challenge of the 60's*. Washington, D.C.: National Association of State Teachers Associations, 1961.

———: "Current Trends in Curriculum Planning—Their Implications for Music and the other Arts," *Music Educators Journal*, September, 1963.

Sand, Ole, and Miller, Richard I.: "New Goals in Instruction," *California Teachers Association Journal* 59:25–28, May, 1963.

———: "Curricular Innovations," *The Bulletin of the National Association of Secondary School Principals* 47:120–123, May, 1963.

———: "Perspective on National Studies in the Disciplines," *Journal of Secondary Education* 38:27–33, January, 1963.

Tyler, Ralph W., and Miller, Richard I.: "Social Forces and Trends," *NEA Journal* 51: 26–28, September, 1962.